Real Time II

Real Time II is about the most intriguing and basic question in metaphysics: what is time? Does it really flow or does it just seem to? How do past, present and future differ? Why can we only act and have experiences in the present? Why can we not see the future, or affect the past – or can we: is time travel possible? How does time differ from space? What gives it its direction?

All these questions are answered in this book, which is a complete reworking of D. H. Mellor's influential 'new tenseless theory of time', developed in his *Real Time* (1981). While defending and developing the themes of that book in the light of later work in metaphysics, semantics and cosmology, Mellor gives new accounts of what statements about the past, present and future mean and what makes them true, of the nature of change and causation, and of what distinguishes time from space, gives it a direction and makes backward time travel and circular time impossible.

The core of D. H. Mellor's view of time remains his thesis that while time itself cannot flow – and events cannot move from future to present to past – our need to live in time compels us to think and act as if it did. From his new arguments for these two views he extracts a complete metaphysics and semantics of time which will set the terms of the philosophical debate on time for the next twenty years, as *Real Time* has done for the last twenty.

D. H. Mellor is Professor of Philosophy at the University of Cambridge, and a Fellow of Darwin College Cambridge and of the British Academy. He is the author of *The Matter of Chance*, *Matters of Metaphysics*, and *The Facts of Causation*, which is also published by Routledge.

International Library of Philosophy

The history of the International Library of Philosophy can be traced back to the 1920s, when C. K. Ogden launched the series with G. E. Moore's *Philosophical Papers* and soon after published Ludwig Wittgenstein's *Tractatus Logico-Philosophicus*. After this auspicious start, the series has been edited by A. J. Ayer, Bernard Williams and Ted Honderich. Now under the joint editorship of Tim Crane and Jonathan Wolff, the ILP will continue to publish the best of original research in philosophy.

Related titles in the ILP include:

THE FACTS OF CAUSATION
D. H. Mellor

A MATERIALIST THEORY OF THE MIND
D. M. Armstrong

MIND, METHOD AND CONDITIONALS
Frank Jackson

G. E. MOORE: SELECTED WRITINGS
Edited by Thomas Baldwin

THE SCEPTICAL CHALLENGE
Ruth Weintraub

Real Time II

D. H. MELLOR

ROUTLEDGE

London and New York

First published 1998
by Routledge
2 Park Square, Milton Park, Abingdon, Oxon, OX14 4RN

Simultaneously published in the USA and Canada
by Routledge
270 Madison Ave, New York NY 10016

Transferred to Digital Printing 2006

Typeset in Times by the author

British Library Cataloguing in Publication Data
A catalogue record for this book is available from the British Library

Library of Congress Cataloguing in Publication Data
A catalogue record for this book has been requested

ISBN 0-415-09780-0
0-415-09781-9 (pbk)

For Derek, Amanda and Dorothy

and The Free Press

Contents

'But does this mean, I hear you cry, that we can no longer look forward to the future that is to come? Certainly not!'

'What about the workers?'

'What about the workers, indeed, Sir.'

— PETER SELLERS, 'Party Political Speech' (1958)
written by Max Schreiner

Preface

I once hoped that this book could be a modest revision of my *Real Time*, first published in 1981 by Cambridge University Press. But it should always have been obvious that this was a forlorn hope. Changes in my own views and the flood of new work in the philosophy of time – see for example Oaklander and Smith (1994) – have forced me to rewrite that book almost completely. While enough of its main claims and arguments survive to justify calling this book *Real Time II*, this is a new and self-contained work. So to avoid distracting readers by noting changes in the body of the work, I shall, for the record, summarise the main ones here.

In *Real Time* I followed the custom of calling temporal locations like past, present and future 'tenses', while distinguishing them of course from the corresponding forms of English verbs. However as failure to observe this distinction still vitiates much philosophy of time, I here call these locations '*A*-times', adapting McTaggart's (1908) now standard distinction between his *A* and *B* series, which I explain in chapter 1. For the same reason I now call my theory of time a '*B*-theory' and my main opponents '*A*-theorists'. The terms 'tensed' and 'tenseless' I confine to their original, proper and trivial grammatical uses.

In chapter 2 I make more explicit what all serious *A*- and *B*-theorists mean by debating the 'truth conditions' of beliefs about the past, present and future. A common but vacuous use of 'truth condition', which lets beliefs have both *A*- and *B*-truth-conditions, can easily make our debate look pointless. But it is not. For what both parties mean by a belief's truth condition is its so-called 'truthmaker', i.e. what in the world *makes* it true. What we disagree about is whether *A*-facts or *B*-facts – in the substantial sense of 'fact' for which I now argue explicitly – make temporal beliefs true. This is a real issue, for if *B*-facts do this job, *A*-facts do not; and if they do not, then they do not exist, since this is what they exist to do.

In *Real Time* I defended the token-reflexive view that an *A*-proposition like '*e* is present' is true at a *B*-time *t* if and only if a token of it – e.g. a statement of it, or someone's belief in it – at *t* would be true. But Quentin Smith (1993a chapter 3) and others have shown that this cannot cope with propositions like 'there are no tokens now', which can be true even though they can have no true tokens. So in chapter 3 I now advocate the simpler view that '*e* is present' is made true at *t* by *e*'s being located at *t*, and similarly for other *A*-propositions.

Chapter 4 contains a new response to Arthur Prior's (1959) claim that *B*-theorists cannot make sense of people thanking goodness that something, e.g. a pain, is past. My old response was shown to be inadequate by the late and sadly missed Murray Macbeath (1983), who also showed me how to correct it. Following him I now exploit the fact that whenever we thank goodness for something's being past, what makes us do so is not that it *is* past but that we *believe* it is; so if, as I argue, we *B*-theorists can say in *B*-terms what any such *A*-belief is, and what makes it true, we can make as much sense as *A*-theorists of our gratitude for (or any other propositional attitude to) the truth of any *A*-proposition.

Spatial analogues of *A*- and *B*-theories are developed in chapter 5 much as in *Real Time*. The main addition is a short section (for which I am indebted to Sir Martin Rees) showing that modern cosmology does not, as some *A*-theorists suppose, undermine objections to *A*-theories based on the special theory of relativity. Far from yielding a privileged reference frame and hence absolute simultaneity across space, its uniform treatment of the expansion of the universe implies that there is no such thing.

In chapter 6 I answer an objection in David Kaplan's (1989) to my theory that a sentence like 'Jim races tomorrow' means a function from any time *t* to its truth condition at *t*, namely that Jim races the day after *t*. Among *B*-theorists the issue is merely terminological – should this function or its values be called the sentence's 'meaning'? – but here it is more than that. For by taking it for granted that *A*-sentences are made true by *B*-facts like Jim's racing on 2 June, rather than *A*-facts like Jim's racing tomorrow, Kaplan begs the question against *A*-theorists, as I do not.

To my development and defence of McTaggart's argument against *A*-facts in chapter 7 I have added a rebuttal of Michael Tooley's (1997) new theory of time. This admits only *B*-facts, while denying, unlike most *B*-theories, that they all exist at all times (on the grounds that *B*-facts about an event *e* come to exist only when *e* does), so that the universe of facts grows over time. This I argue, besides contradicting relativity (as Tooley admits), can appeal only if we confuse *e*'s being *located* at *t* with its *existing* at *t*. Even if the former is what makes '*e* exists at *t*' true, *e*'s existence at *t* will still make both '*e* exists' and '*e* exists at *t*' true at all times.

The *B*-theory of change in chapter 8 differs in one major way from that given in *Real Time*. There I argued that any changeable property *F* (e.g. a temperature) of a thing *a* is a relation *a* has to any *B*-moment *t* when it is *F*.

I am now persuaded that this is wrong. However, I still reject the orthodox *B*-alternative that *F* is a property of a temporal part of *a*, namely *a*-at-*t*, since I still deny that things, as opposed to events, have temporal parts in any serious sense. I argue instead that *a*'s being *F* at any *t* is a *B*-fact whose only constituents are *a* and *F* – the time *t* being not a constituent of this fact but merely its temporal location. This, by making *F* what it seems to be, a non-relational property of *a* itself, stops changes in *a* reducing either to *a*'s being differently related to different times or to different temporal parts of *a* having different properties. That in turn shows why change, so understood, has no spatial counterpart, thus making time as much the dimension of change on my *B*-theory as it is on any *A*-theory.

In *Real Time* I took Davidson's (1980 essay 7) view of causation as a relation between particular events. Now, for reasons given in my *The Facts of Causation* (1995 chapter 9) and summarised here in chapter 9, I think causation, if it relates anything, relates facts, like the fact at *t* that *a* is *F*. This simplifies my *B*-theory of the relation between causation and time, notably by putting the causation of stasis – *a*'s being *F* at a later *t′* because it is *F* at *t* – on a par with that of change. It does however require a parallel treatment of the earlier–later relation, as holding between facts rather than between events or times. This is argued for in chapter 10.4, where I infer on the one hand that events cannot be spacetime points or regions, and on the other, with Leibniz (1717), that it makes no sense to imagine everything happening ten minutes later, say, than it actually does.

The main argument of chapter 10 is that causation is what distinguishes time from space and gives it its direction; in short, that time is the causal dimension of spacetime. Much of this argument follows *Real Time*, but there are three important additions. In §3 I dispose of apparent cases of simultaneous causation. In §5 I show how time's being the dimension of causation makes it also what Kant (1781 B50) calls 'the form of inner sense'. (This supersedes a related but weaker argument in *Real Time*.) And in §6, influenced by Robin Le Poidevin (1991 chapters 5–8), I show why the need for causation to preserve the identity of a thing through changes in its properties restricts change to the causal dimension of spacetime.

In chapter 11 I amplify my rebuttal in *Real Time* of the still widely-held view that it is not causation but irreversible processes which give substance to the difference between *earlier* and *later* and thus give time its direction. I also simplify my causal explanation of our experience of the direction of time (as an accumulation of memories, of memories of memories, and so on) and my demystification of forward time travel.

The case in chapter 12 against causal and hence timelike loops differs from that in *Real Time*. There it derived from Michael Dummett's (1964) argument against backward causation. I have now replaced that argument's epistemic assumptions with the assumption, argued for in chapter 2 of *The Facts of Causation*, that effects have chances, with and without their causes, which are real possibilities of their occurring in the relevant circumstances. (Thus for Jim's smoking, C, to cause him to get cancer, E, his metabolism must give him chances of getting cancer both if he does and if he does not smoke.) I also argue for my previously tacit assumption that, as all agree, a causal relation has only two terms. This requires the fact that C causes E, and so E's chances with and without C, to be logically independent of C's causes, and so in particular of C's chances with and without E. But I show that, if there were causal loops, these chances would not be independent; so there can be no such loops, and therefore neither backward causation nor circular time. This, on my reading of chances as real possibilities, validates the old but much-maligned objection to backward time travel: namely, that if Dr Who, say, could travel into his past he could kill his grandmother in her infancy and so make his trip impossible, which is absurd. And so it is.

I owe much to many people for ideas and arguments about time and related matters that have influenced the contents of this book. Relevant work in English published after *Real Time* is included in the Bibliography. Besides those mentioned above, I am especially indebted to the work and comments of L. Nathan Oaklander, and also to Alexander Bird, Jeremy Butterfield, Max Cresswell, Kenneth Denbigh, Heather Dyke, John Earman, David Farmer, Jan Faye, William Grey (formerly William Godfrey-Smith), Katherine Hawley, Mark Hinchliffe, Ian Hinckfuss, Arnold Koslow, John Perry, David Lewis, E. J. Lowe, John Lucas, Graham Nerlich, Eric Olson, Laurie Paul, Huw Price, Graham Priest, Hans Reichenbach, Peter Riggs, Gonzalo Rodriguez-Pereyra, David Sanford, Kieran Setiya, Larry Sklar, Jack Smart, Joseph Wayne Smith, Paul Teller, Michael Tooley, Susan Weir and Jamie Whyte.

Finally, I wish to thank Tim Crane, and Adrian Driscoll and his colleagues at Routledge, for their patience in awaiting the long-overdue completion of this book and for their help in publishing it, and Gonzalo Rodriguez-Pereyra for preparing the Index.

Cambridge
March 1998

Introduction

Like its ancestor, *Real Time*, this book is about such of the metaphysics of time as follows from settling the basis in reality of our distinctions between past, present and future. One way and another that covers most of time's metaphysics, including the following questions. What makes a statement that something is past, present or future true or false? What is it to have the thoughts that such statements express, and why do we have them? How do we know when they are true: what tells us whether something is past, present or future? Why do we only ever act and have experiences in the present, affect what is future and see what is present or past? Could there be exceptions to this: could a time machine let us see the future or affect the past? What, even in time machines, makes everything outside us keep moving from our future to our past via our present, i.e. what makes time flow? What has the flow of time to do with change, why has it no spatial analogue, and what does this fact tell us about how time differs from space? All these questions will be answered in the course of settling the status of past, present and future.

There are of course other metaphysical questions about time, and three of them at least I shall not try to answer. Is time continuous, dense or discrete? What makes time intervals differ or be the same in extent? Has time a beginning or an end? These questions are too independent of those I shall discuss, and too large, to be tackled here. (The last turns too much on cosmology, the second on how far the measurement of time depends on conventions, and the first on the logic of infinity.)

On the questions I shall discuss I noted in my 1981 Introduction to *Real Time* that the literature was then so vast and various that I could not do it justice succinctly without obscuring the argument I wished to present. The situation has not changed. If anything, the flow of philosophical works on time, if not of time itself, has grown since then. In writing this book I have taken account of it, and of my own changing views, in the ways indicated in the Preface. But it is no more feasible now than it was then to discuss all the works on time and related matters that I have read and been affected by. So now as then I hope that the fewness of my references will not be taken as a sign of ignorance or arrogance. On the contrary, it means that I take my main points, if disputed, to be so common in the literature as to be by now public property. So as before I trust that no offence will be taken by, or on behalf of, those whose well-known work I adopt, adapt or reject without explicit acknowledgement.

This book in short is not a guide to the philosophical literature on time. Like *Real Time*, it is a self-contained, argued exposition of a theory of time many of whose points are already familiar to philosophers. As before, its aim is simply to develop and defend the theory in plain terms and to show how ramified its consequences are. There if anywhere lies its claim to be read. So, to fortify that claim, I will now sketch the main points I wish to make, in case they are obscured by the detail of ensuing chapters.

My answers to the main questions I tackle are as follows. There is in reality no such thing as being past, present or future. By this I do not mean that it is never true to call an event *e* past, present or future: that would be absurd. The question is, what makes a statement like '*e* is past' true when it is true, namely at any time later than *e*? There are two answers to this question. One is that at any such time *e* has the property of being past. This is what, in McTaggart's (1908) now standard terminology, I call the '*A*-theory' view. My own '*B*-theory' view is that what makes '*e* is past' true at any time *t* is the fact that *e* is earlier than *t*. Similarly, what makes '*e* is present' true at any *t* is *e*'s being located at *t*, and what makes '*e* is future' true at any *t* is *e*'s being later than *t*.

This *B*-theory entails that there are no such *A*-properties as being past, present or future, since *e*'s being past, present or future at *t* is by definition what makes '*e* is past', '*e* is present' or '*e* is future' true at *t*. So if, as the *B*-theory says, that is not what makes these *A*-statements true, these *A*-properties do not exist. Compare for example 'Nobody is smaller than a flea'. What makes this true is not that there *is* such a person as Nobody, who is smaller than a flea, but that *no* person is that small. So there is no such person as Nobody, since if there were all true instances of 'Nobody is *F*' would by definition be made true by Nobody's being *F*. As that is not what makes any such statement true, there is no such person.

But why is no true 'Nobody is *F*' made true by something's – Nobody's – being *F*? The reason is that to make all such statements true Nobody would need impossible combinations of properties. Not only for example would Nobody have to be smaller than a flea, he and she (Nobody is both male and female ...) would also have to be larger than a galaxy. But as nothing can be both smaller than a flea and larger than a galaxy, there can be no such person. So every true 'Nobody is *F*' must be made true, as it obviously is, by something else, namely the fact that *no* person is *F*.

Similarly, if less obviously, with '*e* is past', '*e* is present' and '*e* is future'. These *A*-statements cannot consistently be made true when they are true by *e*'s having the *A*-properties of being past, present and future – or so McTaggart argued. I agree with him, and will defend and update his proof of this in chapter 7. This is why I say that there are no *A*-properties, and that our *A*-statements need other truthmakers. And then it is obvious what their truthmakers are, namely those given above by the *B*-theory.

Unfortunately not everyone accepts McTaggart's proof. So to win the day as well as the argument we *B*-theorists must press other objections to *A*-theories of time. One is that important consequences drawn by many *A*-theorists from events being past, present or future conflict with modern cosmology, which makes simultaneity at a distance relative to an arbitrary choice of so-called 'reference frame'. For a star like Sirius, about ten light-years away, this means that no frame-independent fact fixes which Sirian events within a twenty year span are simultaneous with your reading of this sentence and therefore present. This poses no problem for those *A*- and *B*-theorists who think it is always true to say of any actual event, whenever it occurs, that it exists. But most *A*-theorists (and some *B*-theorists) say that nothing exists until it is present, and for them, modern cosmology poses a real problem, since no one can seriously take existence to be relative to an arbitrary choice of reference frame.

Besides pressing objections to *A*-theorists, we *B*-theorists must dispose of their objections to us. One, dealt with in *Real Time*, is that *A*-statements cannot be translated by *B*-statements. Thus '*e* is past', said at *t*, cannot *mean* that *e* is earlier than *t*. For if '*e* is earlier than *t*' is ever true it is always true, while '*e* is past' is true only after *e*; and obviously no two statements can be synonymous if one can be true when the other is false. But this does not stop the fact that *e* is earlier than *t* making '*e* is past' true at *t*. Compare for example 'I live in Cambridge' said by any person *x* (where '*x*' is a name like 'Hugh Mellor', not like 'me'). This cannot *mean* that *x* lives in Cambridge, for if '*x* lives in Cambridge' is true, it is true whoever says it, whereas 'I live in Cambridge' is only true if said by a Cambridge resident. Yet no one can deny that the truthmaker for 'I live in Cambridge', said by any *x*, is that *x* lives in Cambridge.

We *B*-theorists need not then make the hopeless claim that *A*-statements are translatable by *B*-statements. Yet despite this we can still say in *B*-theory terms what *A*-statements mean. For all I need to know in order to understand and use the sentence '*e* is past' is that it is true at any time *t* if and only if *t* is later than *e*. Similarly, all I need to know to understand and use 'I live in Cambridge' is that this is true if and only if a resident of Cambridge says it. So on the orthodox view of a sentence's meaning, as what we must know in order to be able to understand and use it, what 'I live in Cambridge' means is a *function*, from any person *x* to its truthmaker if said by *x*, namely that *x* lives in Cambridge. Similarly, I say, what the *A*-sentence '*e* is past' means is a function from any *B*-time *t* to its *B*-truthmaker at *t*, namely that *t* is later than *e*; and similarly for '*e* is present' and '*e* is future'.

This kind of *B*-theory, giving a semantics as well as a metaphysics for *A*-statements, has been called 'the new theory of time', to distinguish it from older *B*-theories that try to translate or dispense with *A*-statements. My *B*-theory does neither. For not only, as we have seen, does it show why *A*-statements are untranslatable, it also shows why we need the *A*-beliefs these statements express. The reason is that we need such beliefs to make us act successfully when our success depends, as it nearly always does, on our acting only at certain times. I know for example that it is no use shopping when the shops are shut. So I shop only when, and because, I believe they are open, i.e. open *now*. If this *A*-belief of mine is true, I will succeed in shopping, and if it is false I will fail. This is a quite general link between belief and truth: truth is that property of beliefs which makes the actions they combine with our desires to cause succeed, i.e. achieve the objects of those desires. So if an action's success depends on when it is done, its causes must include a belief which is not always true and which we therefore try to have only when it *is* true. But as we have seen, being true only at certain times is the mark of an *A*-belief, since all *B*-beliefs that are true at all are true always.

This is why no agent, human or animal, that acts on its beliefs, and must act at certain times to get what it wants, can do without *A*-beliefs. But then we agents must be constantly changing our *A*-beliefs, especially our beliefs about what is happening *now*, in order to try to keep them true. These changes in us, mostly prompted by our senses, are what make us think of time as flowing, even though it does not flow. For without such properties as being past, present and future, time cannot flow, i.e. make events change from being future to being present and then to being past. But time need not flow for things to change in other ways, by having other incompatible properties, like different temperatures, at different times. And that includes me changing my *A*-belief that *e* is future successively for the incompatible *A*-beliefs that *e* is present and that *e* is past. This sequence of *A*-beliefs is a real process of change – but only in me, not in *e*. Changes like this are the psychological reality behind the *A*-theorist's myth of the flow of time.

This is why our undeniable experience of time flowing is no evidence that time really does flow. Nor does the undeniable fact that all our actions and experiences occur in the present support the *A*-theory. For on a *B*-

theory it is true by definition to say, at any time t, of anything at t, that it is present. So in particular it is always true to say or think, whenever we do or experience anything, that this action or experience of ours is present. The confining of all our actions and experiences to the present is not a real constraint on their location but a mere tautology, like my inability to be anyone but me or anywhere but here.

This account of the presence of experience also explains how we can tell whether an event is past, present or future. No B-theory can admit that these non-existent properties of events are perceptible, and indeed they are not. We cannot for example refute someone who claims to see the future in a crystal ball by pointing to the visible pastness of the scene it shows, since there is no such thing. Whether it is past or future, the scene will *look* the same. Nor can the look of a supernova tell us directly how long ago it happened. That we must infer from its independently known distance and the speed of light, which tells us how much earlier it is than our experience of seeing it – and hence, since we are seeing it in the present, how past it is. Similarly with the terrestrial events which, as we see them, we take to be happening almost *now*, because the light we see them by takes so little time to reach us. This is what tells us that most of what we are seeing is, for all practical purposes, present.

How can we tell when events are future? We cannot tell this by seeing them, and not just because being future is not a visible property of events. For while an event is future we cannot see it at all, since the future is by definition later than the present, seeing something (or perceiving it in any other way) is always an effect of what is seen, and causes always precede their effects. But if this link between the causal order of events and their time order stops us seeing directly that an event is future, it can enable us to tell this indirectly, as when we predict the future effects of our present actions or of the other present events that we can now see.

The link between time and causation also enables B-theorists to explain why it is that, although – or rather because – we can see the past, we cannot affect it. To do so, of course, this link must be, as it is, consistent with a B-theory of time. But consistency is not enough: to be adequate, our theories of causation and time must between them explain why the link holds. Many philosophers explain this by using the time order of events to fix their causal order, defining a cause as the earlier of two causally related events. I do it the other way round, using an independently defined causal order to fix the time order of all events, even of those that are not related as cause to effect.

This enables me to meet several other challenges to B-theories of time. First, it lets me distinguish time from the dimensions of space, and define its direction, not as that in which time flows but as that of causation. For while a cause often has effects in the same place as itself, or in any spatial direction from it, this is never so in time. A causal definition of time order explains all this by requiring a cause's effects to occur in the same temporal direction from it, namely later. This can then be, and I argue is, what makes time differ from space and gives substance to its direction, i.e. to the difference between being earlier than something and being later than it.

Second, we can use the causal machinery of memory to show why the time order we perceive in the world, and in our own experiences, must generally coincide with that given by the causal order of events. By doing so I show in particular how a causal definition of time, and of time order, entails the success of Kant's famous definition of time as 'the form of inner sense', i.e. as the dimension in which our own experiences are ordered.

Third, if time is the dimension of causation, the need for causation to preserve the identity of a thing as its properties change shows why, since causes and effects cannot be simultaneous, there can be no spatial analogue of change. This in turn, by explaining why only temporal and not spatial variations of properties can be changes, meets the most persistent objection to *B*-theories, namely that only the *A*-theory's flow of time can account for the essentially temporal nature of change. That is not so: the dimension of change must also be the dimension of causation.

Finally, I can explain why no one can affect the past or recall the future. This might seem to follow directly from a causal definition of time order, but in fact it does not. For the definition does not itself rule out the causal and hence temporal loops that would let us affect our past by letting us travel back in time. Suppose for example Dr Who's time machine TARDIS could travel back in an hour from 2045 to 1945. Then he could recall in 1945 what he had seen and done an hour earlier in 2045, and those events could affect events in 1945, e.g. by causing a fashion for futuristic scarves of the kind he decided in 2045 to wear.

Why can this not happen? The classic answer is that, if it could, Dr Who could, e.g. by killing his infant grandmother, cause himself never to leave in 2045 (by causing himself not to exist), thus causing a contradiction, which is impossible. Although this answer has convinced few philosophers, it is in fact correct, as I shall show in the last chapter. To find out why – and why I make the other claims outlined above – now read on ...

1 *Past, present and future*

1 The question about time

The great question about time is what past, present and future are and how they differ from each other. The differences seem striking and profound. In the past is everything we have seen and done; in the future everything that has not yet happened or been done, none of which we can yet see; and in the present lie all our experiences, thoughts and actions. We plan for the future because we might affect it, while we know the past is out of reach. This is why it makes sense to think what to do tomorrow, but not what to have done yesterday: the time to think of that was the day before, when what is now yesterday was still future. And having thought what to do, we can only do it now: while the time for action is future we can only await it, and once it is past it is too late.

These ideas about past, present and future are central to our concept of time. But they are not self-evidently right. They want explanation, and while they lack it they will not want for sceptics. Modern physics especially has so altered our views of space and time that some would now set no metaphysical bounds to it. Thus even if no one now hopes to square the circle, some still think for example that we might affect or even revisit the past. To dispel such nonsense we must see more clearly what time is, and in particular what past, present and future are. To make that clear is the main object of this book.

To show what time is, I must start by assuming something about it, since even metaphysical bricks need some factual straw. And if in the end some of my assumptions will have to go, others will survive more or less intact. These of course I shall recommend as I go, since on their credibility that of my case will ultimately rest. But I shall not try to prove that everything I claim is either necessary or undeniable, since my aim is simply to tell the truth about time. Therefore, because necessity interests me mainly as a source of truth, and I do not claim to be infallible, I shall waste no time rebutting merely conceivable objections to what I have to say: doubt and disbelief are not worth trying to dispel unless they are both real and credible.

2 *A*-times

I shall start by introducing some useful terminology and stating some obvious facts. First, for the time being I shall mostly call all past, present or future entities, other than times, 'events'. This is for brevity, and not because I think that events properly so-called (like World War II) do not differ from past, present or future facts (like France having a king), people (like David Hume) or things (like the Crystal Palace). Some of these differences I shall discuss in chapter 8.1, but until then I mean what I say about events to apply also to temporally located facts, people and things.

Then there is the obvious fact that pastness and futurity come by degrees. Past events are not all equally past, nor are future events all equally future. Eighteenth-century events were present before nineteenth-century ones, and that makes them more past. Thirtieth-century events will become present only after twenty-ninth-century ones, and that makes them more future. The time order of the world's events is that in which they become present, thus forming what McTaggart (1908) called the '*A* series'. But his term, though now standard, is ambiguous. It may mean either the sequence of what I shall call '*A*-times', defined by how much earlier or later they are than the present, or the sequences of events located at those times. Since, as we shall see, the difference matters, I shall call the former sequence the '*A*-time scale', or '*A*-scale', reserving '*A*-series' for the latter.

There is of course more to the *A*-scale than the mere order of *A*-times. Next Friday not only succeeds last Friday, it does so by seven days, i.e. by just as much as it precedes Friday-week. *A*-times thus have a measure that reflects how fast the events located at them succeed each other in the present, and also how long those events *are* present. Thus David Hume, who was present on earth for sixty-five years, now occupies sixty-five past years of the *A*-time scale. Other entities last less long: a wedding may be present for less than an hour. But neither people nor weddings are instantaneous: we can no more locate either at a single moment than we can locate them at a single spatial point.

I shall therefore not restrict *A*-times to *A*-moments, but will include intervals of them, whose order, inclusions and overlaps will be entailed by those of the moments they contain. *Last year* precedes *this year* because every *A*-moment in it precedes every *A*-moment in this year; *next week* includes *next Monday* because every *A*-moment in next Monday is also in next week; and so on.

Which *A*-times may we credit an event with at any given time? It is natural to give events any *A*-time that spans them, as when we say that a wedding happened *last week* or *last year*. But I shall also need to refer to *the A*-time of an event, and by this I shall mean its *shortest A*-time, the one whose end-points are the first and last *A*-moments at which the event was, is or will be present.

So much, for the time being, for my basic *A*-scale terminology. In adopting it, I am making no great claims for *A*-moments and intervals, except as a way of stating temporal facts about events. In particular, I do not take this terminology to entail that time could exist without events (although I think it could) or that all *A*-intervals must include shorter ones (although I think they do). Whether time needs events, or is infinitely divisible, are questions that my terminology need not and does not beg.

With these caveats, we may define past, present and future as follows. First, *the past* is the interval of *A*-moments open all the way from the remotest past up to, but not including, the present moment. Then other *A*-times are past if and only if *the past* includes them. Thus *yesterday* is past, as are *last week* and *the first moment of last year*. And any event is past while and only while its *A*-time – the shortest *A*-time that spans it – is past.

Similarly for the future. *The future* is the interval of *A*-moments open all the way to the remotest future and back to, but not including, the present moment. Other *A*-times, such as *tomorrow*, *next week* and *the last moment of next year*, are future because *the future* includes them; and any event is future while and only while its *A*-time is future.

The present is different. It may seem that, to make past, present and future incompatible, we should confine it to the present moment. But then many events, which last some time, would never be present. This problem has prompted the doctrine of the so-called 'specious present', which lets the present encroach a little on the past and the future. But by how much – a minute, a nanosecond? – and what then marks the present off from the non-present past and future? These questions have no good answer; but then they need none, since what is specious is the idea of a specious present, not the present itself.

The right way to define the present is this. In 1943, World War II stretched four years into the past and two years into the future. Yet it was certainly present then, as any combatant would then have testified. So its *A*-time, a six-year *A*-interval including the present moment, should, despite its length, count as present. Similarly we should call any *A*-time 'present', however long it is, if and only if it includes the present moment. That makes *this century* as present an *A*-time as *today* or *this moment*. And so it should, since a centenarian whose *A*-time it is will obviously be present throughout it.

Present *A*-times so defined do indeed overlap and include past and future ones: on any 1 June which is a weekday, *this week* overlaps *last month* (May) and *this year* includes *next month* (July). Yet our definition respects the obvious incompatibility of past, present and future. It stops any *A*-time being both present and past, or present and future, by making present *A*-times include the present moment, and past and future ones exclude it. So nothing that has an *A*-time can ever be both present and past, or present and future. Its *A*-time at any given time either includes the present moment, making it present, or it does not, making it past or future.

This is how, while present events and *A*-times can be of any length, past, present and future remain incompatible properties: no event can have more than one of these temporal properties at once. (I scout the idea, to be dealt with later, that time goes round in a circle, so that what is future is also past.) Yet every event has each of these properties in turn, being first future, then present and then past. This is at once the essential and the most problematic feature of *A*-times, which any account of time must explain.

3 *B*-times

To explain how events move from future to past, we need another way of locating them in time. Dates provide such a way. In 2045, we can say that World War II ended *a hundred years ago*, which is an *A*-time. But we can also say that it ended in 1945, which is a date. Dates are independent of *A*-times, in the sense that any date can, and at some time will, have any equally long *A*-time. The year 2045, like the events in it, was once in the remote future, will eventually be in the remote past, and at some time in between is located at every year-long *A*-time.

So the fact that an event – an eclipse, say – occurs in 2045 says nothing about its *A*-time. The verbal tense I use to give a date may of course imply something about that: 'The eclipse will happen in 2045' implies that it, and 2045, are future, while 'The eclipse happened in 2045' implies that they are past. But we can easily omit this gratuitous *A*-scale information by using or inventing a form of verb which does not vary with *A*-time but can still be used with phrases like 'in 2045' to date events.

Dates thus form a sequence of times that are not *A*-times, because they are not defined by how much earlier or later they are than the present. This sequence, and that of the events which have them, McTaggart called the '*B* series'. As with his '*A* series', I shall remove this ambiguity by calling the sequence of what I shall call '*B*-times' the '*B*-time scale', or '*B*-scale', keeping '*B*-series' for the sequence of events with those times. (By 'times' I shall, like most authors, generally mean *B*-times.)

How are *B*-times defined, if not by how much earlier or later they are than the present? The answer is that they are defined by how much earlier or later the events which have them are than each other. Thus in the Christian calendar 1800 is meant to be the year which contains the events that are between 1800 and 1801 years later than Christ's birth. And the key point about this definition is this: these temporal relations between events never change, unlike their temporal relations to the present moment. For whereas the temporal distance between any event and the present moment is always changing – growing for past events, shrinking for future ones – that between events is always the same: any events that are ever *n* years apart are always *n* years apart. This is why the *B*-times of events, unlike their *A*-times, never change.

The relations of being simultaneous, or more or less earlier or later, are often thought to relate only events and hence only *B*-times. In fact, as I have already assumed, they relate *A*-times too. *Today* is one day later than *yesterday* in exactly the same sense in which 2 June is one day later than 1 June. Having the same *A*-time is being simultaneous in exactly the same sense as having the same *B*-time is. These temporal relations are as basic to the *A*-scale as to the *B*-scale.

This shows how alike the *A*- and *B*-time scales are. They are defined by the same temporal relations, put events in the same order and measure time intervals in the same way. *B*-times, like *A*-times, include moments and intervals of moments, and all my caveats about *A*-moments and intervals apply equally to their *B*-scale counterparts. And none of the questions they raise, about whether time depends on events, or is infinitely divisible, would anyone ever answer differently for *A*- and *B*-times.

The *A*- and *B*-scales are more than alike: they are isomorphic. When any one *B*-moment is present, all times on each scale have counterparts on the other. Thus when it is noon on 1 June 2045, 10 a.m. is *two hours past,* 11 June is *ten days hence,* and *the next decade* is *the twenty-fifties.* All events with those *B*-times have those *A*-times, and *vice versa*; and similarly for all other *A*- and *B*-times. In particular, *the past* is the *A*-time that everything earlier than the present *B*-moment shares, and *the future* is the *A*-time that everything later than that *B*-moment shares.

Thus the link, as well as the difference, between the *A*- and *B*-scales lies in the former's dependence on a present *B*-moment. For just as defining *A*-times by their relation to the present is what marks them off from *B*-times, so the ever-changing identity of the present *B*-moment is what generates the ever-changing but always perfect correlation between *A*- and *B*-times.

The relative priority of the *A*- and *B*-time scales, and hence the nature of time itself, thus turns on the right answer to the question: what makes a *B*-moment present? To answer that question we need to look more closely at the sequences of events located on our two scales, namely the *A*- and *B*-series.

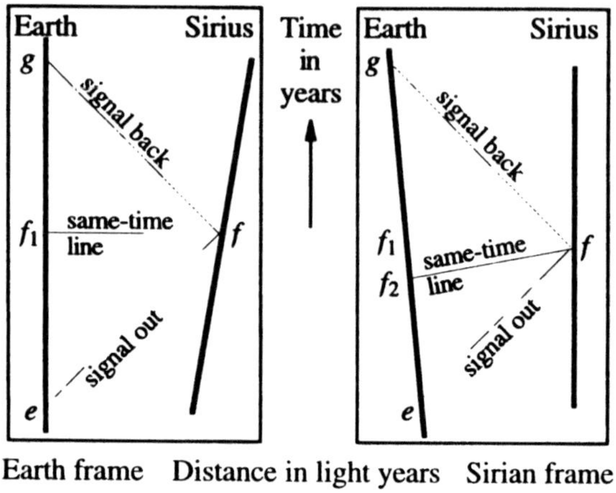

Figure 1

4 *A*- and *B*-series

Although there is just one *A*-scale and one *B*-scale, there are more than one *A*- and *B*-series, i.e. more than one way of giving events *A*- and *B*-times. This follows from the special theory of relativity, to be discussed in chapter 5 in comparing time with space. Here we need only note that special relativity makes the simultaneity of events depend on a choice of so-called *reference frame*. A reference frame may be defined by crediting any given object, that is not accelerating, with a particular absolute velocity, which may be zero. But on the usual reading of relativity, since nothing in the world makes one frame right and others wrong, there is in reality no such thing as absolute velocity. And this matters here because different frames make different celestial events simultaneous with given earthly ones, thereby generating different *A*- and *B*-series, with nothing factual to choose between them.

To see this, suppose we send a light signal to the star Sirius, about ten light years away, and suppose the signal is reflected back to earth. Call the events of the signal's leaving earth, being reflected from Sirius, and being received back here, *e*, *f* and *g* respectively. Suppose also that the earth and Sirius are moving rapidly apart but that neither is accelerating. All this is shown above in Figure 1, in two reference frames, one where the earth is at rest and the other where Sirius is at rest. In the earth's so-called *rest frame f* is simultaneous with an earthly event f_1 and in the Sirian one with an earlier earthly event f_2, thus making *f* present in the first frame when f_1 is, and in the second when f_2 is. This is how, according to relativity, different frames collect different sets of events into the same *A*- and *B*-times and so – since both *A*- and *B*-series are sequences of collections of simultaneous events – into different *A*- and *B*-series.

We shall see in chapter 5 what all this tells us about time and space. Here however we may ignore special relativity's myriad *A*- and *B*-series. For the question here is how *A*- and *B*-series are related to each other, and the answer to that question is the same for every reference frame. For as, in each frame, all events have unique *B*-times, defined by how much earlier or later they are than each other in that frame, there is in each frame only one *B*-series. And to this, at any *B*-moment, there corresponds a single *A*-series of the very same collections of simultaneous events. Thus in Figure 1's earth frame what happens on Sirius on 1 January 2010 – and so what is present there then – is as much a matter of fact as what happens then in Cambridge. This is why, for now, we may ignore special relativity. While we consider how corresponding *A*- and *B*-series are related, we can let those of any one frame stand in for all the rest.

However, even in a single reference frame, while there is only one *B*-series, there are still infinitely many *A*-series. Thus the earth frame of Figure 1 shows only the *A*-series in which f and f_1 are present. But of course these events are not always present in that frame: at earlier *B*-times they are future, and at later ones past. The ever-changing *A*-times of events make each frame's *B*-series correspond to as many *A*-series as there are *B*-moments, since each *B*-moment defines a different *A*-series, namely that in which it is the present moment.

This plethora of *A*-series follows directly from the fact that the *A*-times of events change and their *B*-times do not. That we have seen to be the defining difference between *A*- and *B*-series; and it is an absolute, not a relative, difference. By this I mean that an event's *A*-time varies no less with *A*- than with *B*-times. Take the *A*-time of Hume's death in 1776. This obviously varies from one *B*-time to another: in 1676 it was a century future, sometime in 1776 it was present, and in 1976 it was two centuries past. But it also varies from one *A*-time to another: when, in 2026, Hume's death is 250 years past *this year*, then *three centuries ago* it would have been fifty years future, and so on.

Similarly with the *A*-times of all events, which all vary with both *A*- and *B*-times. But the *B*-times of events vary with neither. Hume died in 1776: at every *A*- and *B*-time that was, is and will be the date of his death. Some philosophers hold indeed that before 1776, when Hume's death was still future, it did not exist and so had no *B*-time at all. But no one thinks it ever had, or ever will have, any *other* *B*-time; nor that the *B*-time of any other event ever varies from one *A*- or *B*-time to another.

The way in which the *A*-times of events vary with *A*-times is the basic subject matter of so-called *tense logic* (so-called because, as all *A*-times vary in the same way, it is almost as general as ordinary logic, and because *A*-times are often called 'tenses'). What makes tense logic worth studying is the fact that iterating the ascription of *A*-times can make truths false and falsehoods true. Thus when 'Jane arrived yesterday' is true, 'Tomorrow, Jane will have arrived yesterday' is false. To recover the original truth, the original *A*-time ascription must be changed: 'Tomorrow, Jane will have arrived two days ago'. And as in this case, so in general: '*e* happened yesterday' always implies 'Tomorrow, *e* will have happened two days ago' (provided of course the universe continues to exist tomorrow).

It should now be obvious why tense logic has no *B*-analogue. The reason is that there are no analogous facts about *B*-times for a 'date logic' to state. Since the *B*-times of events never vary with time, iterating their ascriptions never makes a truth false or a falsehood true. Indeed, the pointlessness of such iteration is so obvious that it sounds very odd to do it at all, to say for example 'On 2 June, Jane arrives on 1 June'. If this says anything, it says the same as 'Jane arrives on 1 June', since if either statement is true, so must the other be. That is all there is to the logic of *B*-ascriptions: iterating them makes no difference to a statement's truth or falsity.

In short, *B*-times are temporally unqualified properties of events, as *A*-times are not; and that, as we have seen, is their only difference. I put their similarity in §3 by saying that the *A*- and *B*-scales are isomorphic. But that understates the matter. For when a given *B*-moment is present, the corresponding *A*- and *B*-times are not just correlated, they are identical. On 1 June, today *is* 1 June, tomorrow *is* 2 June, last month *is* May, and so on. There is at that time no difference at all between those *A*- and *B*-times. So if the *A*-times of events never changed, i.e. if the same *B*-moment were always present, nothing would ever distinguish *A*- and *B*-times. Or rather, since not changing is the mark of *B*-times, there would *be* no *A*-times, and so no *A*-series.

But as events do have changing *A*-times, *A*-times do apparently exist, as well as *B*-times. Yet *A*- and *B*-times are too closely related to be independent properties of events. Which then comes first? I see three possible views. The first is that we live in an *A*-world – events really do move from future to past via the present – which for some reason we also describe in *B*-scale terms. The second is that we live in a *B*-world – events have only *B*-times – which for some reason we also describe in *A*-scale terms. The third combines the other two: events have *B*-times, but there is also a moving present, which gives them real *A*-times.

Those who hold the first or third of these three views, crediting events and *B*-times with real and irreducible *A*-times, I shall call '*A*-theorists'. Those who hold the second I shall call '*B*-theorists'. I am a *B*-theorist. The world, I believe, is a *B*-world: no event is in itself either past, present or future. The *A*-scale is only a way we have of locating events in time; a compelling way, indeed, which we could not do without, but not the way things are in reality. Giving my arguments for this view of time, and a *B*-theory of time that fits it, are the main tasks of this book.

However, before tackling these tasks, there is one objection to any *B*-theory of time which I must deal with immediately. This is that we can directly observe the *A*-times of events, and in particular that we can and do see that they are present. If this was so, it would scotch my *B*-theory at once, since as a good empiricist I will not argue with my senses. Fortunately it is not so; but as it is quite easy in this case to mistake what we see and hear, a little argument is needed at once to prevent the mistake.

5 Seeing *A*- and *B*-times

Whether we can observe events, and what we can observe of them, does indeed depend on their *A*-times. I said in §1 that we cannot observe future events: I cannot yet see or hear any of the events that will happen tomorrow. I shall of course be able to see and hear some of them then; but then they will be present or past. While events are future, they cannot be observed, and this seems itself to be an observable fact about them. But how could it be unless events really are either past, present or future and we can tell by observation which are which?

Yet more tempting is the thought that all our observation occurs in the present. That is, our own experiences, of seeing and hearing things, are given to us in experience as present events and, as such, ones on which our knowledge of all other events depends. Thus we know about past events because, in the simplest case, we now remember having seen or heard them. Our present memory tells us moreover that our experience of seeing or hearing these events, when they were present, was itself a past event. And that, either directly or via our remembering hearing other people's reports, or seeing pictures or other traces of past events, is how in the end we get all our knowledge of the past.

So, the objection will run, experience tells us the *A*-times, not the *B*-times, of events. Our knowledge of the latter we must derive from our knowledge of the former. Thus suppose for example it was now 1976. We would suppose then that Christ was born *1976 years ago*, and know that Hume died *200 years ago*. So then as now the second of these *A*-times is 1776 years later than the first, which is what makes 1776 its *B*-time on the

Christian scale. That, our objector says, is how we assign *B*-times to events, by how much earlier or later their *A*-times are than that of an arbitrarily selected event like the birth of Christ.

Not only, the objection continues, must we derive *B*-times from *A*-times in this way, the latter are in the end all we use our *B*-scale to convey. The only reason we ascribe *B*-times to events is that their constancy gives us a handy way of saying when those events occur. That is why 'Back at two o'clock' is a better sign to pin on my door than 'Back in two hours'. For the latter to stay true, the *A*-time it ascribes to my return would have to alter all the time, e.g. by being shown on a timer set to run down to zero when I come back. By giving my return's constant *B*-time, I avoid that complication. Still, what a reader of my sign wants to know is how soon I will be back, i.e. what the *A*-time of my return is. And to work that out from my sign he must consult his watch to see what *B*-time is *now* and hence what *A*-time two o'clock now has. My timer would have told him that directly, without any reference to *B*-times.

It is tempting to infer from all this that our *B*-scale is only a convenient way of giving information about *A*-times, and that the world we see and are interested in is just an *A*-world. This temptation to adopt an *A*-theory of time should be resisted. For even when our interest in events is what we may call an *A*-interest, that, as we shall see, is a property not of the events themselves but of our interest in them.

For a start, we do not really observe the *A*-times of events. The idea that we do comes from confusing what we observe with the experience of observing it. Suppose I look through a telescope at events far off in space. I see two events and the order they occur in: which is earlier, which later. I do *not* see their *A*-times: the telescope does not show me how long ago those events occurred. What tells me that is whatever theory tells me how far off the events are and how long it takes light to travel that distance. We used, after all, to think that many celestial events were much closer to the earth, and thus much more recent, than we now think they are. So, depending on our theory, we might locate the celestial events we see anywhere on the *A*-scale from a few minutes ago to millions of years ago. Either way they will *look* exactly the same.

In other words, contrary to received wisdom, we see nothing of the *A*-times of these, or of any other visible events. Observation cannot even tell us that what we see is past rather than future. We cannot for example refute someone who claims to see the future in a crystal ball by pointing to the visible pastness of the image: there is no such thing. Our reasons for thinking we cannot see the future rest not on observation but on theory.

But what about the presence of experience itself? If we cannot see the presence or otherwise of the external events we observe, surely we can see that we observe them in the present? To that rhetorical question I can so far produce only the seemingly paradoxical reply that, even when our observations and other experiences tell us truly that they are present, they really are not. I shall try to make good that reply, and remove its air of paradox, in chapter 4. Here it suffices that we can observe the time order of events, other than our own experiences, without observing their *A*-times. For this fact is all it takes to enable us to apply the *B*-scale independently of the *A*-scale.

How do we do that? First, our seeing that one event is more or less later than another is not in general a matter of theory, let alone of a theory of *A*-times. Nothing is easier to see than time order. We see it for example whenever we see something move. Suppose I see a clock's second hand move clockwise, and so see in particular that it passes the numeral '1' before it passes the numeral '2'. To see it move anti-clockwise I should have had to see that these events had the opposite time order: that the hand passed '1' after it passed '2'. And as in this case, so in general. To see that a change of any kind occurs in one way rather than another is to see that some event is earlier, rather than later, than some other event.

I am not of course saying that we can see all cases of events being earlier or later than other events. Some events are not easily seen at all. Others follow on too quickly or slowly for the human eye to catch. Just as we need microscopes to see the shapes of very small things, so we may need time-lapse video-recordings to make very slow changes visible. Nor am I saying that our observations of time order are infallible, or unaffected by scientific theory. Just as we learn that in some lights we are apt to misjudge colours, so we learn that we are apt to misjudge the time order of some events. Thus, having learned for example how much faster light travels than sound, we learn to discount the earlier appearance of lightning, and not to infer that it really occurs before the thunder we hear later.

But normally we simply see how much earlier or later events are than each other, just as we normally see colours. Theories and instruments may extend our ability to see these temporal facts, and may correct our unaided observation of them; although in the end they too depend (like a time-lapse video-recording) on our seeing the time order of *some* events with the naked eye. But whether or not we extend or correct our observations of time order by theories or instruments, the information these observations give us – about how much earlier or later events are than each other – is all we need to know in order to locate events on a *B*-scale.

This means, for example, that beings remote in space could date all our earthly events on the Christian calendar without any idea of how long light took to reach them, or even that backwards causation is impossible. That is, they could see and know enough to set up our terrestrial *B*-scale and apply it to earthly events, without having a clue where these events are in their *A*-scale. This shows how a *B*-series can be known directly, by observing the time order of its events, without reference to any corresponding *A* series.

But then the converse cannot be true: we cannot give events *A*-times independently of their *B*-times. For, as we have noted, *A*-times must satisfy the same earlier–later relations that define the *B*-scale. So whenever one event is visibly earlier than another, i.e. has an earlier *B*-time, it must also have an earlier *A*-time, i.e. be more past. In short, *B*-times constrain *A*-times, not the other way round.

This is not yet to say that the *A*-scale can be dispensed with, or reduced to the *B*-scale. The temporal relations between *A*-times are indeed just those that, by holding between events, define *B*-times. This is why we can derive any *A*-series from a *B*-series just by saying which *B*-moment is present. But it may still be an extra fact about the world, over and above the *B*-times of all its events, that a certain *B*-moment *is* now present. Imagine for example a world identical in all its history to ours except that the present time is now sometime in the eighteenth century. Is there not a real difference between such a world – let us call it an 'eighteenth-century-centred world' – and ours? It is no mean task to show that there is not; yet until I can show this I can hardly deny that the *A*-scale captures a real aspect of the world which the *B*-scale omits. But I, like other *B*-theorists, do deny that; and so in the next three chapters I shall attempt that very task.

2 *Truths and truthmakers*

1 *A*-facts and *B*-facts

The eighteenth century, once present, is now two hundred years past. This does not mean that all eighteenth-century facts about the *A*-times of events like Hume's death (and of *B*-times like 1776) have altered since then. For example, all events and *B*-times that were past then are still past now, and all events that are future now were future then. But most facts about *A*-times have altered in the last two centuries. All nineteenth-century events, which were future in the eighteenth century, are past now. Seventeenth-century events, which were past then, are still more past now; and thirtieth-century events, which are future now, were still more future then. The last two hundred years have seen quantitative if not qualitative changes in the *A*-times of all events and of *B*-times.

How, given all these differences, can we *B*-theorists deny that our actual world, including its past and future, differs from an eighteenth-century-centred world – or rather worlds? For if new *A*-facts mean a new world, there will be one born every moment, which may be a rather less appealing consequence of *A*-theory than a new world every century.

But, appealing or not, to reject this consequence we must distinguish two kinds of facts. There are what I shall call '*A*-facts', contingent facts about the *A*-times of events and of *B*-times. Facts that entail no *A*-facts I shall call '*B*-facts'. These include necessary facts (if there are such things), like the fact that 2+2=4, and also tautological combinations of *A*-facts, like the fact that any event either is or is not past. But here the most important *B*-facts are contingent facts about how much earlier or later events are than each other, and hence about what their *B*-times are; none of which, as we saw in chapter 1, entail any *A*-facts. These are what I shall generally mean by '*B*-facts'.

Do the *B*-facts of eighteenth-century-centred worlds differ from those of our world? Many *A*-theorists think so, since they think that *A*-facts affect what *B*-facts there are, for example that only *B*-facts about past or present events exist. Even some who only accept *B*-facts think that these increase with time, since they think that no events with any *B*-time *t* exist before *t*, thus stripping eighteenth-century-centred worlds of all *B*-facts about nineteenth- and twentieth-century events. So in attacking these rival views I cannot, without begging the question, simply assume that the world's *B*-facts do not vary with time. That will have to be shown.

Some *B*-variation I can allow, at least for the time being. In particular, I can allow the possibility or necessity of a given *B*-fact to vary with time. Thus I can admit that while at any *B*-moment there are many possible futures, there is only one possible past, the actual one. For this is consistent with there being at that moment only one *actual* future, containing all and only the *B*-facts that will eventually be first present and then past. So while, since Napoleon lost at Waterloo in our actual past, he must have lost in the eighteenth century's actual future, he may still have won in a possible eighteenth-century future that is not now a possible past. This shows how *B*-possibilities may vary from time to time even if *B*-actualities do not.

But how can we refute the idea that actual *B*-facts vary, either because events at *t* do not exist before *t*, or because what is future does not exist, or because – as so-called *presentists* believe – only what is present exists? Here we must avoid being misled by the variable spelling of the English verb 'exists'. For if we contrast 'exists' with 'existed' and 'will exist' by defining it as 'is present', we shall make it a mere tautology that only what is present exists. Similarly, to define 'exists before *t*' as 'has a *B*-time earlier than *t*' makes it a mere tautology that events located at *t* – and hence *not* earlier than *t* – do not exist before *t*.

But the authors who think that only what is present or past exists are not peddling mere tautologies. So to be fair to them we must avoid a trivially present-entailing reading of 'exists'. We must credit them with needing better grounds than the variable spelling of an English verb for saying that, before the nineteenth century, that century's events had no reality at all, so that there were no *B*-facts about them. And we must agree that, if these authors are right, eighteenth-century-centred worlds must differ greatly and non-tautologically from ours. For then these worlds will include only those nineteenth-century entities which, like Napoleon I, overlap the eighteenth century, whereas ours includes other nineteenth-century entities, like Napoleon III.

Similarly, on the presentist view, we shall share even fewer entities (and *B*-facts about them) with eighteenth-century-centred worlds, namely only those with *B*-times that span the last two centuries, like England and the earth. But not Federal Germany, which did not exist two centuries ago, nor the Holy Roman Empire, which does not exist now. Nor most of the earth's animal inhabitants, whose lives are too short: so no people, and only a small and shrinking number of giant tortoises.

These consequences of the views I oppose seem to me absurd enough to make entailing their falsehood a strong argument for my *B*-view of time. Yet to be rid of them we shall need all the *B*-facts whose existence they deny. How then can we say what those facts are without begging the question? The answer, roughly, is that the *B*-facts we must identify need not be about what now exists. They need only be consistent with what now exists.

No one can really deny this modest consistency requirement, despite the inconsistency of many time travel tales. Thus if a time-travelling *A*-theorist were to return from the future to disrupt my present typing, that supposedly future *B*-fact would contradict the present fact that my typing is *not* being disrupted. As that is not possible, real time travellers must either avoid doing what is not being done anyway, or switch between worlds where it is being done and worlds where it is not. Whether backward time travel is possible even with such precautions is a very moot point, as we shall see in chapter 12; but even if it is, no one thinks that my typing at noon on 25 July 1997 can both be disrupted (at one time) and not disrupted (at another) in a single world. And none of the views which I am trying, temporarily, to accommodate assume that it can. This is why they do not fill in the eighteenth century's actual future with *B*-facts that differ from those of our actual past, but simply leave it blank.

But then we can add the eighteenth century's future to it, and its past too if need be. To the universally admitted (because then present) *B*-facts of eighteenth-century-centred worlds we can consistently add all *B*-facts about earlier and later events. Those who deny that these facts existed then may read them hypothetically, as what they would have been had they been present. And read in that way no one can deny them. For no one can deny that, even if what is future or past does not now exist, the present is neither what it was nor what it will be. And I am only saying how it was and how it will be: I am simply distinguishing the world's actual history from merely possible variants of it.

There is however one objection to this ploy that I must try to meet at once. It is that if worlds contain even hypothetical facts about their future entities, people in those worlds should be able to refer to them. But King George III could surely not refer to Queen Elizabeth II, as she obviously could to him; and this asymmetry seems to reflect more than the difficulty of knowing facts about the future. For suppose George III did guess many *B*-facts that seem to be about Elizabeth II, including her name. He might still not be referring to her, since his guesses might have been made true, even if she had abdicated, by a sufficiently similar queen of the same name. But Elizabeth II, by contrast, could certainly refer to George III in such a way that if *he* did not do what she said, her remarks would be false, even if he had abdicated and the actual king (also called 'George III') did do what she said.

This contrast suggests to some philosophers that any eighteenth-century-centred world in which George III is present lacks a future Elizabeth II for him to refer to, and also that it lacks any way of referring to her as even a hypothetical future entity. If this is so, then we cannot add to those worlds any *B*-facts about her, since no facts in those worlds could be facts about *her*. Whereas now that she does exist, and can be referred to, there are many *B*-facts about her, which eighteenth-century-centred worlds must therefore lack.

The short answer to this objection is as follows. First, if it assumes that George III could not refer to Elizabeth II *because* she does not exist in his future, it begs the question. So it must infer her non-existence as the reason why he – obviously – could not refer to her. But once we think that she *might* exist in his future, this inability is much less obvious, and anyway has other explanations. For any account of time which, like mine, says that the future exists must explain why we know so much less about it than we do about the past. This I shall do later by saying why we cannot perceive events before they occur. And that in turn will explain why George III could not talk about Elizabeth II. For if no one in his time could perceive anything about her and her times, then even if she does exist in his future, he could not in practice know enough about her to refer to her.

In short, the fact that we cannot perceive the future, even if the future exists, is quite enough to explain why we are rarely able to refer to future entities. And even if the existence of all such entities is denied on other grounds, that need not stop me saying what the *B*-facts about them are. For future entities, like future *B*-facts, can always be specified hypothetically, as whatever entities certain *B*-facts *will* be about when, at some future *B*-time, they are present and hence, on any view, exist.

I conclude that *A*-differences do after all exhaust the factual differences between eighteenth-century-centred worlds and our own, with the proviso that *B*-facts about future (and perhaps past) events may have to be read hypothetically. Subject to this proviso – to be removed in chapter 7.5 – all *B*-facts were the same then as they are now. Then as now, everything is the same at the same *B*-times, with people at all those times seeing, thinking and doing the very same things. Whatever the present time may be, the world remains the same in all these *B*-respects.

Yet my problem remains. Even if no *B*-facts have changed since the eighteenth century, many *A*-facts have. The very few surviving Galapagos tortoises that were young when Darwin's visit to them was still future are now much older, i.e. their births are now much more past. Most of the eighteenth century contained a present king of France, which our world lacks; the English Revolution was only about a century old; the Russian one was more than a century off; and so on and so on. These and many other *A*-differences between then and now are both undeniable and undeniably factual. How can we accommodate them while denying that in reality events and *B*-times have the *A*-times which these differences seem to entail?

Tackling this problem may well seem to be a task both daunting and perverse. That it is not too daunting I shall show in the next chapter by actually doing it, i.e. by giving *B*-surrogates for all the *A*-facts whose existence I deny. But it will take more than that to acquit me of perversity. 'Because it's there' may be a good enough answer to 'Why climb Everest?' but it is hardly good enough here. We cannot disprove the existence of *A*-facts just by finding *B*-surrogates for them. To take a familiar analogy, the idea that the sun goes around the earth cannot be refuted just by showing how the appearance of sunrise and sunset could still be explained even if the earth went around the sun. The heliocentric explanation must also be shown to be the right one. Similarly with my *B*-theory account of past, present and future: I will still have to show that it is right. But I can hardly do that until I have said what it is.

2 Temporal truthmakers

The first step in explaining away *A*-facts is to trade them in for *A*-truths, by which, for a start, I mean true *A*-beliefs, i.e. true beliefs about the *A*-times of events (and of *B*-times). No one will deny that such beliefs can be true or false, nor that which they are depends on when they are held. This means that we must, for example, distinguish believing *now* that an event is *past* from believing in the *past* that it was then *present*. The former I shall call a present *past*-belief, the latter a past *now*-belief, and similarly in other cases. Thus suppose that today is 1 June, the day before my friend Jim's big race. My present future-belief that Jim will race tomorrow differs in type from the future now-belief, that he races today, which I expect to have tomorrow, even if both beliefs are made true by the same fact.

But which fact makes these two beliefs true, the presently existing *A*-fact that Jim races tomorrow, or the *B*-fact that he races on 2 June? That is the question: are *A*-beliefs made true by *A*-facts, as *A*-theorists believe, or by *B*-facts, as we *B*-theorists believe? To enable us to answer that question, I must first say more about truths and how they relate to facts.

The scope of the concept of truth is debatable. Here I shall apply it to beliefs, to statements of them, to sentences expressing them, and to their contents, which I shall call 'propositions' and assume are what sentences expressing beliefs mean. And as anything I can believe I can also doubt, disbelieve, want, fear, hope etc., I shall also take propositions to be the contents of all these other so-called 'propositional attitudes'; as in my doubting if, or disbelieving or desiring that, Jim races tomorrow. But since for present purposes beliefs can usually stand in for other propositional attitudes, I shall mostly ignore the others and consider only beliefs.

I shall take it then that my belief that the earth is round is true if and only if the following are true: a statement of it; a sentence expressing it; and the proposition that is the meaning of this sentence and the content of this belief (and also of such attitudes as disbelief, doubt and desire that the earth is round).

The variety and interdependence of these 'truth bearers' raises obvious questions about which comes first. Do sentences get their meaning from the contents of the beliefs they express, or is it the other way round? What beliefs could we have with no language to state them in? And so on. These are good questions, but not ones that I need to answer. For the issue here is not what the bearers of *A*-truth are – beliefs, statements, sentences or propositions – but what makes them true when they are true. And as the answer to that question will be much the same whatever truth bearers are, stating the issue at first in terms of belief will beg no relevant questions. Whatever makes *A*-beliefs true at any *A*- or *B*-time will also make corresponding *A*-statements, *A*-sentences and *A*-propositions true at that time.

Other questions about the scope of truth are also by the way. Does the concept apply to beliefs about values, or about how probable events are, or about unobservable entities postulated by scientific theories? Does it apply to beliefs whose truth values (true or false) cannot be discovered because they are about events too remote in space or time? These too are questions I need not answer. For even if some *A*-beliefs lack truth values for these reasons, many do not, since they are not about values, probabilities, theoretical entities or events too distant to be seen. It is too easy to tell, and too plainly factual, what century or time it is, what happened last year and (I say) when Jim races, for anyone to deny that *A*-beliefs about these and many other matters are objectively true or false.

Certainly no sensible *B*-theorist denies this. We can all agree with *A*-theorists that many *A*-beliefs have truth values. Indeed most *B*-theorists credit more *A*-beliefs with truth values than many *A*-theorists do. For if *A*-facts about the future are what make future-beliefs true or false, those who deny that such facts exist must also deny that such beliefs are true or false. But this further debate about the scope of truth we may also set aside. For whatever the range of true or false *A*-beliefs, the question about them is the same: is it *A*-facts or *B*-facts that give them their truth values? This is why

I need not defend my use of contentious examples, like my belief that Jim races tomorrow. Readers who deny that this future-belief has a truth value can always substitute some past- or present-beliefs which they do think have truth values. It will make no odds to the argument that follows.

Before starting that argument, however, I must distinguish not only *A*-facts and *B*-facts but two senses of 'fact'. In one sense, of course *A*-beliefs correspond to *A*-facts. This is the sense in which the equivalence,

'Jim races tomorrow' is true if and only if Jim races tomorrow,

is both trivially true and entails that (abbreviating 'if and only if' to 'iff')

'Jim races tomorrow' is true iff *it's a fact that* Jim races tomorrow.

Suppose now we take this to entail that 'Jim races tomorrow' is true if and only if the *A*-fact that Jim races tomorrow exists. No sense of 'fact' in which this follows will settle the dispute between *A*- and *B*-theorists. For this does not tell us what *makes* it true, and hence a fact, that Jim races tomorrow.

In short, accepting this entailment makes our concept of fact as weak as the concept of truth on which

'Murder is wrong' is true iff (it's a fact that) murder is wrong,
'Jim will probably win' is true iff (...) Jim will probably win, and
'Quarks have spin' is true iff (...) quarks have spin

are also trivially true. But if these equivalences are only trivially true, they can hardly show that, for murder to be wrong, Jim to probably win and quarks to have spin, the world must contain objective values, probabilities and theoretical entities. Theories of value, probability and the nature of scientific theory which deny this are not so easily refuted.

Yet however contentious objective values, probabilities and theoretical entities may be, no one denies that many *A*-beliefs are made true by something objective and, among other things, temporal. The question is, what? So in calling our rival answers to that question '*A*-facts' and '*B*-facts' the word 'fact' needs a sense stronger than that in which it is trivially true that

it's a fact that Jim races tomorrow iff Jim races tomorrow.

It is therefore in a stronger *truthmaker* sense of 'fact' that, when it matters, I shall use the word from now on, a sense in which both *A*- and *B*-theorists can agree that

'Jim races tomorrow' is *made true* by a fact P,

while offering different candidates for P.

What are the rival candidates? The nature, constituents and even the existence of truthmaking facts are still in dispute. Even those of us who think there are such things still differ about what to call them. Armstrong (1997), for example, calls them 'states of affairs', whereas I follow most philosophers in meaning by this any possible (or even impossible) fact, e.g. the P that will make 'P' true if it *is* a fact, i.e. is a state of affairs that has the property of 'obtaining'. In *The Facts of Causation* (1995) – *FoC* for short – I call truthmakers 'facta' (singular 'factum') and argue that they are all atomic, i.e. not conjunctive, disjunctive or negative. For suppose 'P' and 'Q' are made true by facta P and Q. Then we need no other facta to make true 'P&Q' or, for any R, 'P∨R' (i.e. 'P or R') or 'Q∨R': P and Q will do that. Similarly, what will make 'P' false and hence '~P' true is that P does *not* exist, not that a negative not-P factum does.

These however are contentious issues which we need not settle here. Here it will be simpler, and beg no questions about time, to write as if conjunctions, disjunctions and negations of facta are also truthmakers and so, to avoid confusion with facta proper, to call them all 'facts'. For all that matter here are the temporal constituents of truthmakers. How the truthmakers of 'Jim races tomorrow', 'Jim and Jack race tomorrow' and 'Jim or Jack race tomorrow' differ is by the way. The only question here is what constituent of their truthmakers makes these future-propositions *temporal*. What are the candidates for that?

The candidates I gave earlier differ less than one might suppose. If today is 1 June, the *A*-truthmaker for 'Jim races tomorrow' is Jim's racing *a day later than today*, while its *B*-truthmaker is his racing *a day later than 1 June*. Both truthmakers include the earlier–later relation, one of the basic temporal relations on which we saw in chapter 1.3 that both *A*- and *B*-time scales rely. So as what matters here is how these truthmakers differ, we can postpone many questions about these relations too, such as what they are (universals? tropes?) and what they relate (events? facts?). For whatever the answers to those questions, they will serve *A*- and *B*-theorists equally well.

The only real difference between *A*- and *B*-truthmakers is that the latter are, as the former are not, limited to *B*-facts. Hence our problem. For if Jim races only on 2 June, the *A*-proposition 'Jim races tomorrow' is true only on 1 June, which is when its *A*-truthmaker (that Jim races tomorrow) exists. But unlike this *A*-fact, the *B*-fact that Jim races on 2 June is always a fact, as I say all *B*-facts are. How then can such facts make propositions true at some times and false at others, as most *A*-propositions are? That is the question we need to answer.

Perhaps we should answer it by denying after all that *B*-facts do exist at all times? Take the idea, mentioned in §1, that *B*-facts only come to exist when the events they are about occur. The idea is meant to let us accept only *B*-facts while denying the existence of the future. For if no *B*-facts about the events of 2 June exist on 1 June, then none can make it true on 1 June either that Jim races tomorrow, i.e. on 2 June, or that he does not; and similarly for all other *A*- and *B*-propositions about the future.

I reject this idea because, as I argue in chapter 7.5, 'Jim races on 2 June' and 'Jim races tomorrow' must surely be true on 1 June if on 2 June an *A*- or *B*-fact makes it true then that Jim races today, i.e. on 2 June. But even if they are not, that will not solve the present problem, to which after all the idea that *A*-propositions need *B*-facts to make them true assumes a solution. For no *B*-fact can be needed to make 'Jim races tomorrow' true unless some such fact is, or is entailed by, what does make this proposition true.

And this is our problem: to show how *B*-facts *can* make *A*-propositions true, a problem that arises only because even *B*-theorists agree that some *A*-propositions *are* sometimes true. But then, as I have already remarked, we may as well assume that 'Jim races tomorrow' is one of them. For if it can be true, then we *B*-theorists need to say what *B*-facts would make it so; and even if it cannot, then it can still stand in for *A*-propositions that can.

So it will beg no question here to assume, as I do, that all *B*-facts exist at all times. But then our problem remains: how can they be truthmakers for *A*-propositions that are not always true? Of course the truth values of some *A*-propositions do *not* vary, such as the tautological falsehood 'Jim does and does not race tomorrow'. (Classical logic makes this an *A*-proposition because, unlike the tautological truth 'Jim does or does not race tomorrow', it entails *A*-facts, since it entails everything.) But tautological truths and falsehoods pose no problem in any case, because they need no truthmakers; since whatever makes any 'P' true or false will also make 'P∨~P' true and 'P&~P' false.

Nor is our problem made easier by the fact that even some contingent *A*-propositions are always false or always true, as 'Jim races tomorrow' and 'Jim does not race tomorrow' would be if Jim never raced at all. Some such propositions we must consider later. But not here, simply because these are not the ones that pose the problem: it is varying truth values that we *B*-theorists find hard to handle, not unvarying ones. This is why I make Jim race on some days but not others, in order to make the truth of 'Jim races tomorrow' vary with time, as the existence of its *A*-truthmaker does.

It is because *B*-facts, unlike *A*-facts, do not come and go that no single *B*-fact can make 'Jim races tomorrow' true at some times and not at others. But if not one, then how many *B*-facts does it take to give an *A*-proposition its varying truth values? The answer is as obvious as it is discouraging: it takes as many *B*-facts as there are times at which an *A*-proposition can have independent truth values. In our case this means one *B*-fact a day throughout Jim's life. For because his racing (or not) on one day entails nothing about his racing (or not) on any other day, it takes a new *B*-fact to make 'Jim races tomorrow' true or false each day. Where then are we *B*-theorists to find all these facts, and how can they make this *A*-proposition true when it is true and false when it is false?

3 *Tokens and times*

1 Tokens

To find enough *B*-truthmakers for *A*-propositions we need to invoke the well-known distinction between *types* of entity and *tokens* of those types. A token of a type is a specimen of it in the sense in which Jim is a specimen of humanity. And as for humanity, and other natural and social types, so for mental and linguistic ones. Take for example the type and token senses in which 'the' and 'the' in this (token!) sentence are, and are not, the very same word.

The type–token distinction can be applied to all the truth bearers of chapter 2.2: not only to sentences but also to beliefs, statements and propositions. In the sense in which others may share my future-belief that Jim races tomorrow, this belief is a type, whose tokens are my belief, your belief, Jim's belief, etc., that Jim races tomorrow.

But these are not yet the tokens we need. For I can have this future-belief at one moment and not at another; as indeed I should, since if the belief is true today, it will be false tomorrow. This means that the tokens we need are people (and animals, if they have beliefs) believing things at given moments. My believing at noon on 1 June that Jim races tomorrow is one such token, my believing the same thing four hours later is another, and so on.

This makes the belief-tokens we need facts: my believing a proposition 'P' at a given *A*- or *B*-moment *t*. And if *t* is a *B*-moment, then even if 'P' is an *A*-proposition, my believing it at *t* is a *B*-fact, entailing nothing about how much earlier or later anything is than the present. Thus my believing at any *B*-moment of 1 June that Jim races tomorrow is a *B*-fact, entailing nothing about the *A*-time of Jim's race, 1 June or anything else.

That *B*-facts can be tokens of *A*-propositions is crucial to the *B*-theory. I must stress therefore that this is not a peculiarity of token beliefs, arising from the fallibility which, for most P, stops my believing 'P' entailing P. For even if I *know* on 1 June that Jim races tomorrow, which does entail that he races then, my token knowledge is still not an *A*-fact. For first, all it entails is that my belief that Jim races tomorrow is true, not that what *makes* it true is an *A*-fact, which is the point at issue. And second, my knowing on 1 June that Jim races tomorrow entails only the *B*-fact that he races on 2 June. It does not entail the *A*-fact that he races *tomorrow*, for it does not entail that 1 June is today. And as for knowledge and belief, so for doubt, disbelief, desire, fear and all other propositional attitudes. Whatever my attitude to the *A*-proposition that Jim races tomorrow, my having that attitude at any *B*-moment is a *B*-fact, not an *A*-fact.

So much for mental tokens of propositions. What about statements, the entities postulated to distinguish what is said (a statement) from what we use to say it (e.g. a sentence)? We have good reason to draw a distinction here, since we can use different sentences, e.g. in different languages, to say the same thing. But since we could draw the distinction just as well by saying that different sentences can express the same proposition, this is a weak reason for postulating statements as well as propositions. And the other common reason for postulating statements is worse than weak, for it begs a relevant question. This reason is that we can use a sentence to say different things in different contexts, e.g. 'It's a girl' said of different babies. But taking 'Jim races tomorrow' to make different statements on different days (on 1 June that he races on 2 June, on 2 June that he races on 3 June, etc.) assumes that those statements are *B*-statements. For if 'Jim races tomorrow' makes an *A*-statement, it makes the same statement every day, namely that Jim races tomorrow.

So to avoid begging the question against *A*-theorists I shall assume that we can make both *A*- and *B*-statements, and thus that to every possible belief type, i.e. to every proposition, there corresponds a statement type. But then we may as well call statement types 'propositions', which is what from now on I shall do, keeping the word 'statement' for any spoken or inscribed (written, printed or otherwise displayed) token of a proposition.

In calling all such tokens 'statements' I am ignoring such questions as: how can different sentences in different languages (or contexts) be used to make the same statement; must we use sentences to make statements, or can they also be made by gestures, pictures or other non-linguistic means? Important as they are, these are not questions we need to tackle here. Here we need only note one difference between inscribed and spoken statements.

Take my 'Back in two hours' sign of chapter 1.5. This inscription, like my belief that Jim races tomorrow, has a truth value at every moment of its existence – a truth value which may, and does, vary from time to time. So here, as with beliefs, the tokens we need are not the inscription itself but the sign's bearing this inscription at particular moments. Its doing so at noon is one such token, its doing so at 1 p.m. is another, and so on.

But now suppose that at noon, as I leave, I *say* 'Back in two hours'. This token utterance takes time (say two seconds) and none of its temporal parts (e.g. my utterances of the words it contains) makes any statement at all. So my saying that I will return in two hours generates only one token of that proposition. Unlike the written sign, it does not generate an infinity of tokens, each with its own truth value, at every moment of its short life. Yet it too has a *B*-time (a two-second interval about noon) on which its truth value depends: if I utter it about two hours before I return it will be true; otherwise it will be false.

In short, all tokens, however diverse, of any *A*-proposition 'P' for which we need *B*-truthmakers, have *B*-times which (given 'P') fix their truth or falsity in any given world. Can these *B*-facts, about when tokens occur, give us the *B*-truthmakers we need: can they give all *A*-propositions the variable truth values which we know they have? Let us see.

2 Token-reflexives

If I say on 1 June that Jim races tomorrow, that statement is true; if I say it again on 2 June, that statement is false. Here are two tokens of the same *A*-proposition, one true and one false. What *B*-facts give them these truth values? The answer is obvious: my first statement is true because I make it a day before Jim races; my second is false because I make it on some other day.

So the *B*-fact that makes a token of 'Jim races tomorrow' true seems to be this: the fact that the token is located a day earlier than the day on which Jim races. And similarly for every *A*-proposition 'P' about any event *e*. Roughly speaking,

> any token of 'P' is true if and only if it is as much earlier or later than *e* as 'P' says the present is than *e*.

Thus if 'P' says that *e* is *n* units (seconds, years, ...) *future*, then its tokens are true if and only if they are *n* units *earlier* than *e*. (In our example the unit is a day and *n* is 1.) Similarly, if 'P' says that *e* is *n* units *past*, then its tokens are true if and only if they are *n* units *later* than *e*. Thus my saying or thinking 'Jim won two years ago' (where the unit is a year and *n* is 2) is true if and only if I say or think this in the second year after Jim's victory.

If 'P' says that *e* is *present*, then its tokens are true if and only if they are *simultaneous* with *e*. More precisely, if 'P' says that *e* has a present *A*-time that is *n* units long, then its tokens are true if and only if they are within *n* units of *e*. Thus if I say 'Jim is training this week' (where the unit is a week and *n* is 1), my statement is true if and only if I say it in a week when Jim is training.

This shows how the truth value of a token *u* of an *A*-proposition about an event *e* varies with facts about how much earlier or later *u* is than *e*. These facts moreover are all *B*-facts, since they entail no *A*-facts: '*u* is *n* units earlier/later than *e*' entails nothing about the *A*-time of either *e* or *u*. So we *B*-theorists can use these facts to say what makes (tokens of) *A*-propositions true or false. And since these are facts about the very tokens whose truth values they give us, we can be sure of having as many of them as we need. So far then so good for this so-called *token-reflexive B*-theory of what gives *A*-propositions their truth values.

3 'Here be (no) tokens'

But not good enough, because a token-reflexive theory gives some *A*-propositions the wrong truth values. Imagine a time *t* when no one has written or is thinking or saying anything, i.e. when there are no tokens of any proposition; and consider the now-propositions

'There are tokens now' and
'There are no tokens now',

which I shall call '*u*' and '~*u*' respectively. At *t*, '*u*' is false and '~*u*' is true. Yet obviously no *token* of '*u*' can be false at any time, and no token of '~*u*' can be true. For whenever there are any tokens of any proposition, '*u*' and its tokens are true and '~*u*' and its tokens are false. So when '*u*' is false and '~*u*' is true, the token-reflexive tale of what makes these now-propositions true or false will give the wrong answer.

But if propositions like '*u*' and '~*u*' refute my token-reflexive *B*-theory, they also refute its *A*-theory analogue. For while '*u*' could easily be false and '~*u*' true *today*, no tokens of '*u*' and '~*u*' could have those truth values today. These now-propositions can no more have token-reflexive *A*-truthmakers than they can have token-reflexive *B*-truthmakers.

So the fact that '*u*' and '~*u*' cannot have token-reflexive truthmakers does not support *A*-theories of time against *B*-theories. Nor is the issue that this fact raises limited to now-propositions. It arises also for their personal and spatial analogues, like 'Jim races *me*' and 'Jim races *here*', whose tokens are also made true or false by facts about those tokens, namely *who* produces them and *where*. The issue is a general one, about how the truthmakers of all these so-called *indexical* propositions are related to those of their tokens.

Take the personal analogues, '*v*' and '~*v*', of '*u*' and '~*u*', namely

'I am thinking or saying something' and
'I am thinking and saying nothing'.

While '*v*' is all too often false and '~*v*' true, no one can think or state '*v*' falsely or '~*v*' truly. Similarly with the spatial analogues of '*u*' and '~*u*', '*w*' and '~*w*', which say respectively (at some given time)

> 'There are tokens here (now)' and
> 'There are no tokens here (now)'.

'*w*' is often false and '~*w*' true, since at any one time there are many places devoid of writing, statements and thoughts. But no token of '*w*' can ever be false anywhere, and no token of '~*w*' can be true; since wherever there are any tokens of any proposition, '*w*' and its tokens are true and '~*w*' and its tokens are false. So wherever '*w*' *is* false and '~*w*' *is* true, a token-reflexive account of their truth values will be wrong.

Why do these facts raise an issue? It is after all obvious when, why and how these propositions differ in truth value from their tokens. Why does it matter that they do so? The reason is that tokens of a proposition 'P' *should* be true if and only if 'P' is true – and so, in particular, should be true when, of whom and where 'P' is true. This is so because, as we shall see in chapter 6, we want to have token beliefs that are true, i.e. true of us when and where we have them. (I may wish that my belief 'P', e.g. 'I have lost the race', *was* false, but that is wishing 'P' false, not wishing to disbelieve 'P' when 'P' is true.) Yet how are we to get true beliefs if not by believing propositions that are true of us when and where we believe them? And even when, as in lying, we want to utter falsehoods, how can we do so if not by stating propositions which we believe to be false of us when and where we state them?

These are of course rhetorical questions. For what *is* the truth value of any token *u* of any proposition 'P' if not the truth value which 'P' has for whomever produces *u* when and where they do so? As I do not see what else a token's truth value can be, I do not see how propositions can differ in truth value from their tokens. So it is just as well that, despite appearances, the propositions we are considering do not do so. For what makes any token *u* of '*u*' ('There are tokens now') true at any time *t* is precisely that *u*'s being located at *t makes* '*u*' true at *t*. And similarly in our other cases. None is a proposition 'P' whose tokens ever differ in truth value from the truth value 'P' itself has in the circumstances, including the existence of a suitably located token of 'P'.

This is all very well, but it does not solve our problem. It does not alter the fact that whatever makes '~*u*' true at any *A*- or *B*-time *t*, it cannot be what would make '~*u*''s tokens true then, since those tokens are never true. What then does make '~*u*' true at a time *t* when, as it says, there are no tokens? The answer can only be a fact about *t* itself, namely that there are no tokens at *t*; and similarly in the personal and spatial cases. What makes 'I am thinking and saying nothing' true of any person *x* is that *x* is thinking and saying nothing, just as what makes 'There are no tokens here' true at any place *s* is that there are no tokens at *s*.

These answers however invoke more than tokens. They invoke times, people and places, as well as propositions. And while no one denies that there are people, and I have defended propositions in chapter 2.2, times and places remain contentious. But not, fortunately, on grounds that matter here. Thus suppose for example we agree with Leibniz that to talk about time and space is really to talk about temporal and spatial relations between events. This is not to deny that times and places exist, merely to say that they depend for their existence and identity on events, whose temporal and spatial relations define them.

Nor does it matter if we agree with Einstein that it takes an arbitrary choice of reference frame to fix which events throughout space are located at a local time *t* (and which events throughout time are located at a present place *s*). For as we saw in chapter 1.4, it remains a fact in any one frame which events are located at *t*, and so whether 'There are no tokens now' is true at *t* in that frame; and similarly for 'There are no tokens here' at *s*. So we can again ignore special relativity by letting any one reference frame stand in for all the rest.

In short, I see nothing in Leibniz or Einstein to stop us replacing tokens with times in our truthmakers for *A*-propositions. Nor does our doing so beg the question against *A*-theorists since, as we have seen, 'There are no tokens now' refutes *all* token-reflexive accounts, *A*- and *B*- alike, of what makes *A*-propositions true. So *A*-theorists too need times – *A*-times – to give *A*-propositions *A*-truthmakers. Thus, if we let *t* be either an *A*- or a *B*-time, we can all agree to replace the token-reflexive theory of §2 with:

> any *A*-proposition 'P' about any event *e* is made true at any *t* by *t*'s being as much earlier or later than *e* as 'P' says the present is than *e*;

and similarly for its personal and spatial analogues. This theory of what makes *A*-propositions true, because it indexes their truth values to times, we may call an indexical theory. And its *A*- and *B*-variants both give all *A*-propositions, including 'There are no tokens now', their right truth values at all times. Thus if *A*-theorists can say in these indexical terms what makes *A*-propositions true, so can *B*-theorists.

4 Necessary pasts and possible futures

So far, again so good. But so far we have only considered *A*-propositions about what has happened, is happening or will happen in the actual world.

Yet, as I noted in chapter 2.1, we may also believe that some future events are *possible* which in the end do not occur, as when a coin toss which could land heads in fact lands tails. Or we may believe that once a toss has landed tails, its not landing tails is no longer possible, i.e. that an actual event's becoming past makes it *necessary*. How can a *B*-theorist account for these so-called 'modal' *A*-propositions?

The *B*-theory of these propositions has a hard and an easy part, and here fortunately we need only the easy part. The hard part is to say in what senses of 'necessary' and 'possible' the past is necessary and some non-actual futures are possible. This I shall do in chapter 12 by showing why backward causation is impossible, thus giving a clear sense in which the past must be as it actually is: namely, that nothing present or future could now affect it. But as our present actions, and other present events, can and do affect many future events, the latter are not in this sense necessary; which means that, in the corresponding sense of 'possible', some alternatives to them are possible.

But I need not press this reading of past necessity and future possibility here, since we *B*-theorists can accept any reading of these modalities which admits the actual future argued for in chapter 2.1. All we must deny is that events being necessary or possible in this sense depends on whether they are past or future, i.e. earlier or later than the present. And it is easy to see what we should say instead, namely that events being necessary or possible at any *B*-moment *t* depends on whether they are earlier or later than *t*. Thus if a tossed coin lands tails at 4 pm on 1 June, its landing tails is (in the relevant sense) necessary at all later and no earlier times, while its landing heads is (in the relevant sense) possible at all earlier but no later times.

In short, given a *B*-truthmaker for the now-proposition that *t* is present, *B*-theorists are as well able as *A*-theorists to say what makes all past events necessary and some non-actual future events possible. These modal *A*-propositions pose no new problem for the *B*-theorist.

5 Complex *A*-propositions

But if modal *A*-propositions pose no new problem, complex non-modal ones may. Suppose it is now 1 June, and consider the English sentence

> 'A week tomorrow, Jim *will have raced* a week ago'.

This sentence uses the so-called 'future perfect' form of the verb 'to race' to say that, in eight days from now, Jim's race, whose present *A*-time is *tomorrow*, will have the different *A*-time *one week past*. And this is true, because the *A*-time of Jim's race, like that of all events, is always changing.

English uses the simple present and past tenses of verbs to say what *A*-times events have now. Thus 'Jim *races* tomorrow' says that his race is *now* future, 'Jim *raced* yesterday' says it is *now* past, and so on. But when we want to say what *A*-times events had in the past, or will have in the future, we use more complex forms, like the future perfect. And then, since the *A*-times of events are always changing, we must say *when*, if not now, these events have the *A*-times we ascribe to them. We can use *B*-times to do this, saying for example that Jim's race will be a week past *on 9 June*. Or we can use *A*-times, as in the sentence above: Jim's race will be a week past *a week tomorrow*.

This is why, as we noted in chapter 1.4, ascriptions of *A*-times can be iterated. Fortunately for the tense logic mentioned there, if not for us, they can also be *re*iterated, endlessly. For not only does the first *A*-time we ascribe to an event keep changing, so do all the others. Not only is 'Jim races tomorrow' only true today, so is 'A week tomorrow Jim will have raced a week ago'. Yesterday, for example, both of those *A*-propositions were false, so that it is now false that

> yesterday, Jim would, in *eight* days time, have raced a week ago.

What is now true is that

> yesterday, Jim would, in *nine* days time, have raced a week ago.

This gives us two more *A*-propositions, which are now respectively false and true and include not two but three *A*-times. The way their truth values change from day to day then generates *A*-propositions with four *A*-times; and so on, endlessly.

To study all these *A*-propositions systematically, tense logicians express them in a standard way, prefixing ascriptions of *A*-times successively to a core now-sentence. Thus the core in our example,

> 'Jim races today',

might be elaborated into

> 'Tomorrow, Jim races today',
> 'Yesterday, tomorrow, Jim races today',
> 'A week ago, yesterday, tomorrow, Jim races today',

and so on. All these *A*-propositions have, at any *B*-moment, definite truth values. So when (on 2 June) 'Jim races today' is true, the elaborations of it listed above are respectively false, true and false. So *B*-theorists need to find even more *B*-truthmakers for all these propositions.

It would be nice if we could avoid this chore by noting that in real life, as opposed to tense logic, no one iterates *A*-time ascriptions more than once or twice. And we should certainly be suspicious of these endless sequences of propositions, which seem to be generated more by the system than by the world. But the suspicion, though sound, gives us no immediate respite. For even if complex *A*-propositions never are stated or believed, they could be; and if they were, their tokens would have truth values – namely, as we saw in §3, those that the propositions tokened have at those times. So, tokened or not, these propositions all need truthmakers.

As we cannot of course hope to find all the *B*-truthmakers we need case by case, we shall need a recipe to generate them automatically. Fortunately we can adapt a recipe, devised by tense logicians to provide simple *A*-truthmakers for any complex *A*-proposition 'P', which goes like this. First, state 'P' in the standard form, with a string of *A*-time-ascriptions prefixed to a simple now-sentence. Take the first of these ascriptions and imagine the present *B*-moment that much earlier or later. Starting from there, repeat this for all the other *A*-time-ascriptions in turn. Then ask if the core now-sentence is true when the present *B*-moment has the *A*-time arrived at in this way. If it is, 'P' is true now; if not, not.

Suppose for example we start by putting our original proposition,

'A week tomorrow, Jim will have raced a week ago',

into the standard form

'A week hence, tomorrow, a week ago, Jim races today'.

Then suppose the present *B*-moment shifted forward a week, then forward a day, and finally back a week, i.e. to tomorrow. Finally, ask if 'Jim races today' is true tomorrow. As Jim does race tomorrow, the answer is 'Yes'; so the original statement comes out true, as it should.

From this *A*-recipe, which tells us what *A*-facts would make 'P' true *now*, we can derive the following *B*-recipe, which will tell us what *B*-facts would make 'P' true at any *B*-time t. First, take the *B*-time t_1 that is as far from t as the first *A*-time ascribed in 'P' is from the present. Next, take the *B*-time t_2 that is as far from t_1 as 'P''s second *A*-time is from the present; and so on. Then ask if 'P''s core now-sentence is true at the *B*-time arrived at in this way. If it is, 'P' is true at t; if not, not.

Thus suppose we ask whether

'A week tomorrow, Jim will have raced a week ago', i.e.
'A week hence, tomorrow, a week ago, Jim races today'

is true on 1 June. We first go forward a week to 8 June, then on a day to 9 June, and back a week to 2 June. Is 'Jim races today' true on 2 June? As Jim races on 2 June, the answer is 'Yes'. So our *B*-recipe makes 'A week tomorrow, Jim will have raced a week ago' true on 1 June, as it should – and as our *A*-recipe does when 1 June is today.

And as in this example, so in general. If our *A*-recipe can give simple *A*-truthmakers for *A*-propositions of any complexity, so can our *B*-recipe. It is obvious, moreover, that the two recipes are always consistent. That is, at any present *B*-time *t*, the *B*-recipe will give any *A*-proposition the same truth value at *t* that the *A*-recipe gives it *now*.

Of course the fact that both our recipes always give the same answer may not prove that the answer they give is always right. But for once in a way a general proof that it is would be superfluous. For, as we have noted, no one in real life thinks or states very complex *A*-propositions. We therefore lack any independent awareness of when they are true with which to judge the deliverances of our recipes. On the contrary, with propositions as complex as my example, we have to work out if and when they are true – which we do by using the recipes I have just given. So these *must* give us the right answer, since they are what we use to decide what the right answer is.

In particular, therefore, our *B*-recipe tells us how to find *B*-facts that will give any *A*-proposition the right truth value at any time. But this of course does not show that *A*-propositions are in fact made true by *B*-facts rather than *A*-facts, let alone that there are no *A*-facts. There may still be other reasons for believing in *A*-facts; and there are, as we shall now see.

4 *The presence of experience*

1 The *A*-theory of clocks

That it is now (as I write) the twentieth and not the eighteenth century is a fact of experience, over and above all *B*-facts about the temporal times of events, which nothing in chapter 3 captures. I call it a fact of experience for two reasons. First, it is the fact that my experiences are in the twentieth century which tells me that the twentieth century is present. Second, what makes my experiences tell me this is the self-evident fact that they themselves are present. How can we *B*-theorists explain this fact away?

The problem we face is well illustrated by a puzzle, adapted from Lewis Carroll, which invites you to choose one of two clocks, after being told only that one is never right and the other is right just twice a day. It is not much of a choice, but presumably you choose the second. But you are wrong, since the first clock goes perfectly (but is five minutes slow), while the second does not go at all!

But what is wrong with a stopped clock? After all, not only is it right twice a day, it also tells you *when* it is right, namely at the very time it stopped, say 2.15. So you can see what it says, and you know when that is true. What more do you want?

The answer is, of course, that you want to know if it is 2.15 *now*. No one needs to look at a clock to see that 'It is now 2.15' is true at 2.15, since that *B*-fact is always a fact. That is not what we look at clocks to see. We look at clocks to see which *B*-time is now present, say 2.15. But the fact that 2.15 is present is an *A*-fact, and therefore not always a fact. So good clocks will only state such facts when they *are* facts. That is why their hands need to keep moving and why, if we want them to tell us the time, we need to look at them when that time is present.

It seems then that *B*-facts cannot capture what a stopped clock does not tell us and a good clock does. Of course a good clock is one that says '2.15' at 2.15, '3.30' at 3.30, etc.: those *B*-facts may still be what makes everything it says true. But these *B*-facts do not tell us which of these *B*-times is the *present* time, which is what we want to know. And that is what makes the slow clock better than the stopped one: its now-statements of the present time are only ever five minutes out, whereas the stopped clock is mostly hours out. That is why we, rightly, prefer the former to the latter.

This is the obvious, *A*-theory, solution to our puzzle. The stopped clock is worse because it is worse at telling us the now-facts about what time it is which we want to know. Yet how can this matter if, as we *B*-theorists claim, no such facts exist? To answer that question we must first solve another puzzle, set for *B*-theorists by Arthur Prior (1959).

2 'Thank goodness that's over'

Suppose that, after a painful experience, I say with relief 'Thank goodness that's over'. I seem to be thanking goodness for an *A*-fact, the fact that my pain is past; and this is why I thank goodness after the pain, not during it. Can *B*-theorists make sense of this?

Prior says not. When I say 'That's over', referring to a pain, the *B*-fact which we *B*-theorists say makes this statement true is the fact that I make it later than the pain. But why should I be glad of this fact, which on my *B*-theory was as much a fact during the pain as after it? Not only that, but I could have known it during the pain, since I could have decided then that I would say 'That's over' afterwards. So if this is the fact I am glad of, I could have been glad of it while I was still in pain! But that is absurd. So it must be some other fact that I am glad of and thank goodness for, a fact which does not exist until after my pain – namely, the *A*-fact that my pain is now past.

The conclusion seems clear: *B*-truthmakers fail to capture a key aspect of experience, namely its temporal *presence*. Being present seems to be essential to any experience, i.e. essential to its being an experience. To give only the *B*-times of my experiences, without saying which of them I am having *now*, is to leave out precisely what makes them experiences. Once over, a pain is no longer a pain, since nothing can be a pain, or an experience of any other kind, unless it is present. A past pain can only be a pain in the dispositional sense that it would be a pain if it were present. But as it is, it is just a retired or Emeritus pain. It is no longer in business as the real experiential article, which is why I am glad of its pastness; for its becoming past has stopped it being painful.

It seems then that experiences, if nothing else, must have *A*-times, namely present ones. But if experiences have *A*-times, other events will have them too, since their *A*-times follow from how much earlier or later they are than our present experiences. And this restores all the *A*-facts that distinguish the many worlds of chapter 2 which differ from ours only in the *B*-times that are present in them.

There may be a slide from personal to objective time. A time traveler would not dread the objective future that contains him in pain since that's in his personal past!

I'm glad that my current experience is not of that time. But this is susceptible to Prior's objection. Actually I think it works.

Not only are all our pains and other experiences present, they tell us that they are present. I argued in chapter 1.5 that we do not in general perceive the *A*-times of events. But the *A*-times of experiences we do perceive: we perceive them to be present; and on this fact depends all our knowledge of the *A*-times of other events. When I see a past event, like a solar flare, it is the perceptible fact that my seeing it is present which tells me that the flare must be as far into the past as it is earlier than my seeing it. And as in this case, so in others: it is the self-intimating presence of our observations that enables us to infer the *A*-times of the events we observe, and enables me in particular to see that the century I am presently writing in is not the eighteenth but the twentieth.

So the presence of experience is the crux. We need a credible *B*-theory of it before we can begin to deny the existence of *A*-facts. Such a theory I shall now give, beginning with an answer to Prior's objection which I owe to Murray Macbeath (1983).

The key to this answer is the fact that what makes me glad that my pain is over is not that it *is* over but that I *believe* it is over. With pain of course the two go together, because we generally believe that we are in pain when and only when we are in pain. This being so, then if at any *B*-time *t* I believe I am now in pain, this now-belief can be made true by the *B*-fact that I am in pain at *t*; and similarly if I believe at *t* that I am not now in pain.

Similarly again with my belief that my pain is past. We generally have these past-beliefs only when they are true, i.e. only after we have been in pain. But we may not have them even then, since we may have forgotten being in pain. So suppose I have forgotten that. Then even though my pain is past, I will not believe that it is, since I will have no belief about it at all. But then I will not be glad, and so will not thank goodness, that my pain is past. (Its ending may still give me a feeling of relief, and I may be glad and grateful for that, but this is not being glad that anything is *past*.) And as in this case, so in all cases. The immediate cause of our being glad of any *A*-fact (or *B*-fact, come to that) is not the fact itself but our belief in it.

In saying this I am not of course trying to identify being glad of a fact with being glad that one believes it. Being glad has a propositional content, in this case the *A*-proposition that my pain is past, which differs from the proposition that I believe my pain is past. And it is the former proposition, not the latter, that must be true at *t* for my gladness at *t* to be well-founded. But this *A*-proposition can still be made true at *t*, and hence my gladness well-founded, by the *B*-fact that my pain is earlier than *t*.

This is how we *B*-theorists can explain when and why people are – and should be – glad of the fact that a pain is past, even though we deny that there are any such facts. We can do this because in order to do it we need say only what makes people believe that a pain is past when they do, what makes this past-belief true when it is true, and why they should be glad that it is true. And *B*-theorists can do all this as well as *A*-theorists can, as follows.

Because my pain and its absence are self-intimating, and I have some short-term memory, my pain's ending at *t* causes me to believe thereafter that my pain is past, to be glad that it is, and therefore to say 'Thank goodness that's over'. The *B*-fact that I do this only after my pain is what makes the past-belief that my 'That's over' expresses true, and that fact in turn is what makes the gladness which my 'Thank goodness that's over' expresses well-founded.

But is this explanation really good enough? How, in particular, does it explain my being glad only *after* my pain and not during it? There is, as we have seen, an *A*-theory answer to this question (when a pain is past it is no longer a pain) which we *B*-theorists cannot give. What can we say instead?

Nothing *a priori*. But then nor can *A*-theorists, since the fact which they think we cannot explain – that only the end of a pain makes us glad – is not always a fact. What shows this is the existence of masochists, who are *not* gladdened by the end of a pain they have been enjoying. On the contrary, what they are glad of, and will therefore thank goodness for, is the start of a pain, not the end of it. And since I could be a masochist, even if I am not, it is a contingent fact that I am glad only after my pain and not earlier. But then it takes more to explain this fact than the necessary truth that the end of my pain makes it past. To this the *A*-theorist must add the claim that my belief that my pain is past, and hence my gladness that it is, is caused by my pain's becoming past. But why must this *A*-fact be the cause of my past-belief and hence my gladness? My believing just after some *B*-time *t* that my pain is past, and hence my being glad then that it is, could be caused by the *B*-fact that my pain ends at *t*. That would explain equally well why, not being a masochist, I thank goodness only when, and because, I believe (truly) that my pain is past. But then we *B*-theorists can cope with Prior's case as well as *A*-theorists can. So it provides no argument against us.

3 The necessary presence of experience

This answer to Prior gives us the element we need to explain away the presence of experience. That element is the self-awareness which makes both the presence and the absence of pain self-intimating. For in order to thank goodness that my pain is past I must not only believe that I *was* in pain, I must also be aware that *now* I am not in pain, or at least not in as much pain as I was. This kind of self-awareness is the element we need.

My awareness at any *B*-time *t* of being fairly free of pain is a conscious now-belief about my experiences at *t*, namely that they are not (very) painful. This awareness, since it is conscious, we may call an experience, even though that is debatable. For even if it is an experience, we will still need to distinguish it from the experiences of which it is an awareness. The distinction is easy to overlook, simply because our experiences differ from other events, almost by definition, as those of which we are directly aware. But in what follows the distinction will be crucial, which is why I stress it.

The link between experience and awareness may make us seem to be always and infallibly aware of the experiences we are now having. Thus while I may miss or mistake the colour of my pen, I can hardly miss or mistake my experience of seeing it – rightly or wrongly – to be red. My awareness of this experience is so closely tied to it that they are easily confounded. Yet we must distinguish them, if only because I need not have conscious now-beliefs about all my experiences. For example, while we are rarely if ever *in* pain without noticing it, we are often free of pain without noticing it. My being free of pain need not cause me to believe consciously that I am now free of pain, even though, if I do believe it, I am perhaps bound to be right. So if I do have this now-belief at any time *t*, that is an extra fact about me, over and above the fact that I am not in pain at *t*.

To be aware of not being in pain is, I have said, to believe consciously that the experiences I am having now are painless. Now as this now-belief is about my *present* experiences, it will be true at any time *t* if and only if all my experiences at *t* are painless. And similarly for all my other now-beliefs about my present experiences. If I believe at *t* that I am now seeing a red pen, that belief will be true if and only if I am seeing a red pen at *t*.

Now consider my now-beliefs, not about my present freedom from pain or the colours I am now seeing, but about temporal features of my present experiences. Suppose in particular that I believe these experiences to be located in the present. Notice that, for an *A*-theorist, this need not be a tautology. For the ever-changing *A*-times of events, including experiences, require us to ascribe them at a specific time, e.g. the present; which does not of course entail that they too must be present. But then it is not clear why all the experiences I am having now must be located in the present. Why may they not include events that are now past or future?

Thus, far from being a tautology, it seems a striking fact that events can only be experiences while they are present. On this fact, moreover, as we have seen, depends our knowledge of all other *A*-times: it is what lets us infer that the events we see are, as we see them, as much past as they are earlier than our observations of them.

Yet if this is how we infer the A-times of other events, it obviously cannot be how we discover that our experiences are present. Rather, being present must itself be an aspect of experience, something of which we are directly aware. My perceiving that my experiences are present is therefore very like my perceiving them to be painless. On the one hand I need not perceive it, since I can have experiences without thinking about their A-times at all. On the other hand, if I do perceive it, I am bound to be right, as I am when I perceive an experience of mine to be painless. Our perception of the presence of our experience, like that of many if not all its other features, seems to be infallible.

But there is one big, and suspicious, difference between our perceptions of presence and of painlessness. Whereas only some experience is painless, all of it is present. Whoever I am, and whenever I believe my experience to be present, that now-belief will be true. This is the inescapable presence of experience that we B-theorists must explain away. And once we distinguish our experiences from our now-beliefs about them, that is not hard to do.

We know already that, for any event e, the now-proposition that e is present is true just when e occurs: that is this proposition's B-truthmaker. Now take my now-belief that the experiences I am having now are present. This now-belief does not ascribe presentness to all my experiences, past, present and future, only to the ones I am having now, i.e. at the B-time at which I have this belief. But their being so located will automatically make this now-belief about them true. So if these B-facts are what make this now-belief true, then it must be true, since its B-truthmakers stop it being anything else.

This is my B-theory of the otherwise mysteriously inevitable presence of experience. And this theory is not just an alternative to an A-theory of that inevitability, since there is no such theory. For if events do have A-times, I cannot see why the experiences we are having now cannot include events that are now located in the past or in the future. The fact that this never happens can only, on an A-theory, be a brute fact about experience. There is admittedly one A-theory which entails it, namely presentism, which holds that only the present exists and hence in particular that only present experiences exist. But that does not explain why experiences at least seem to differ in this respect from other events, with A-times that include all A-times. For many of the apparently real events we see, notably celestial ones, are obviously past; and all those that we predict or plan are just as obviously future. Only our experiences, beliefs, intentions, decisions and actions seem to be confined to the present. Of this contrast, only the B-theory I have just given gives any explanation.

The fact is that experiences, like other events, are in themselves neither past, present nor future. But we can and do have now-beliefs about them, as we can about anything else, and most of these are by no means trivial. For example, even if I cannot believe I am in pain when I am not, so that my belief that I am now in pain cannot be false, this does not make the proposition that I am now in pain necessarily true. But the proposition that the experiences I am now having are present obviously *is* necessarily true, a fact which *B*-theorists, and only *B*-theorists, can explain, by making it a tautology. We need not suppose, as *A*-theorists must, that its necessity reflects a profound, because inexplicable, restriction on the *A*-time of experience.

4 A *B*-theory of our times

So far so good. Better still, we can now solve all the problems posed in §1, starting with Lewis Carroll's clocks. Imagine first a clock that keeps good time. Although no *B*-facts about the clock itself will pick out the present time, other *B*-facts will do so. Suppose for example I look at the clock at 2.15. Since the clock is right, it says '2.15', a token of the now-proposition 'It is now 2.15'. So if I trust the clock, it will cause me to believe that very proposition. And since it is right, then (ignoring the time that it takes me to believe it) it will cause me to believe 'It is now 2.15' at 2.15, thus causing me to have this now-belief when it is true. This, in *B*-theory terms, is what a good clock does: it causes those of us who look at and trust it to have now-beliefs about the time which are true when we have them. And that, after all, is what we want our clocks to do.

What about Lewis Carroll's clocks? The one that is never right because it runs five minutes slow will cause those who trust it to have now-beliefs about the time that are not far out. That is, even if the most precise now-belief it gives me is false, most of what I infer from it will be true. If I never need to know the time to within five minutes, such a clock will never let me down. But a stopped clock would often let me down dreadfully if I trusted it. At most times of the day, it would give me a now-belief about the time which was so far out ~~it~~ that it would make me miss important engagements completely. This is why a clock that is never more than five minutes out is so much better.

So Lewis Carroll's puzzle does have a *B*-theory solution after all, a solution which also shows why our world need not differ from those where the eighteenth century is present. For the world is really just a good clock writ large, as we can see by asking how a good clock at 2.15 differs from the very same clock an hour later. The answer is of course that no *B*-facts distinguish them, just as no *B*-facts distinguish our world from eighteenth-century-centred ones. So if all facts are *B*-facts, there is only one world, just as there is only one clock, with its events scattered over time, including both the eighteenth and the twentieth centuries.

But among the world's temporally scattered events are people making *A*-statements and having *A*-beliefs at various *B*-times. And of these events, our twentieth-century A-statements and *A*-beliefs have *B*-truthmakers that are centuries later than those of the same propositions' eighteenth-century tokens. This is why tokens of so many *A*-propositions differ in truth value in the two centuries. It is why, for example, all our tokens of 'The present King of France is bald' are false (they occur when France is a republic) while many eighteenth-century ones are true (they occurred when France had a male monarch with a wig). All these tokens of that *A*-proposition, some true and some false, can still inhabit the same world, simply because their different *B*-times give them different *B*-truthmakers and hence their varying truth values. We need no *A*-facts to explain why living in one century differs in so many striking *A*-respects from living in another.

Some, I know, will never accept this *B*-theory of our times. Even if we give them *B*-truthmakers for every *A*-proposition at every *B*-time, they will still ask which of these times is *now*. But to any token of that question we can always reply that its own *B*-time, *t*, is what makes '*t*' the answer to it. No *A*-fact is needed to make that answer true. But then they will ask the same question of our answer: is the time *t now*? An endless regress is possible of such questions and their answers. But the regress is not actual, and it is not vicious, since every question in it has an answer whose truth-maker is the *B*-time of that very question.

Those of us who deny the existence of *A*-facts are often accused of taking an impossibly eternal 'view-from-nowhen' of the world, neglecting our own immersion in the stream of time. But the accusation could more justly go the other way. It is *A*-theorists who fail to take seriously that all events are in time – including all our *A*-beliefs and *A*-statements. For it is the fact that these too have *B*-times which enables the world's *B*-facts to provide all their truth values.

5 *Time and space*

1 Spatial analogues of time

I have not yet shown that nothing in reality is past, present or future, i.e. that there are no *A*-facts. I have shown only that *B*-facts can make any *A*-proposition true when it is true. My *B*-theory of the presence of experience depended on this thesis, as will my later case against *A*-facts. The thesis is essential to any *B*-theory of time and so must be rightly understood. Yet while simple enough, and not new, it is still often misconstrued. In particular, three obvious falsehoods are often inferred from it, which I must therefore show that it does not in fact entail.

The false inferences are these. First, if *A*-sentences have *B*-truthmakers, they must mean the same as the *B*-sentences which state those truthmakers and which we could therefore use to express our *A*-beliefs. Second, if there are in reality no *A*-facts, we should be able to dispense with *A*-beliefs and think and talk only in *B*-terms. Third, since the spatial analogue of the *B*-theory is obviously true, the *B*-theory explains, and may even be entailed by, a key implication of Einstein's special theory of relativity, namely that the four dimensions of spacetime are in reality all alike.

Each of these inferences is false. Most *A*-sentences are not translatable by *B*-sentences; we cannot do without *A*-beliefs; and time is not like space (and relativity does not show that it is). I must show then that *B*-theories of time need not entail these falsehoods, and I shall start with the third. I will need the spatial analogy anyway, in order to show its limitations, and the analogy will then help me to dispose of the other two inferences in chapter 6. For everyone accepts a *B*-theory of space, even though our spatial *A*-talk is as obviously untranslatable, and our spatial *A*-beliefs as indispensable, as their temporal counterparts.

2 *A*- and *B*-places

Since space has three dimensions to time's one, the arrangement of things and events in space is more complicated than it is in time. But this does not stop *A*- and *B*-times having spatial analogues, which I shall call *A*- and *B*-places. It means only that there are three analogues – north–south, east–

west and up–down – of the earlier–later relation. But as it does not matter which or how many of these analogues we take, we may simplify matters by drawing the analogy for two-dimensional arrays of places on land.

My *B*-places will then be the spatial locations shown on terrestrial maps. These places can be given by latitude and longitude, just as *B*-times can be given in years BC or AD. For as in the BC/AD system, latitude and longitude define places by their distance and direction from a given thing or event. The equator and the meridian correspond to Christ's birth, degrees of latitude and longitude to years, and the directions north–south and east–west to earlier–later.

B-places and *B*-times need not of course be given in such comprehensive systems. 'Ten miles north of Cambridge' also picks out a *B*-place, just as 'ten years after the end of World War II' picks out a *B*-time. But however they are picked out, *B*-places and *B*-times are defined by fixed spatial and temporal relations between things and events.

In calling *B*-places 'fixed', I am not denying that people and things can move. The fact that they can does indeed mark a major difference between space and time, related to time's being the dimension of change, including change of place. But we are not yet ready to deal with change. That comes later, and it involves the difference between spatial and temporal *relations*. Here however we need only the analogy between spatial and temporal *locations*, i.e. between places and times. And to this analogy the fact that things can move is irrelevant, for the following reason.

In giving something's *B*-time, I am not saying that it fills the whole of space throughout that time, merely that during that time it is always in some place or other, a place that may vary from time to time. Thus Hume's *B*-time (1711–76) tells us only that throughout that time he is somewhere on earth. Similarly, in giving something's *B*-place, I am not saying that it occupies all of this place for ever, merely that it is at every place within it at some time or other, a time that may vary from place to place. Whether it stays still, occupying all of its *B*-place at once, or moves around within it from one smaller place to another, is immaterial.

Because space has more than one dimension, the *B*-places of things and events can be more convoluted than their *B*-times. Hume's *B*-place, for example, is a web-like region of all the ground he ever stood, sat or lay on (or was ever over or under) in his life. This of course is why we rarely, if ever, think of it: it tells us so little about him. If for example you want to meet my racing friend Jim, it hardly helps to be told where he is at some time or other, which is all that my telling you his *B*-place tells you. You want to know where he is at particular times, say at his home on 1 June, at the races on 2 June, and so on: in short, part of his so-called *world line*,

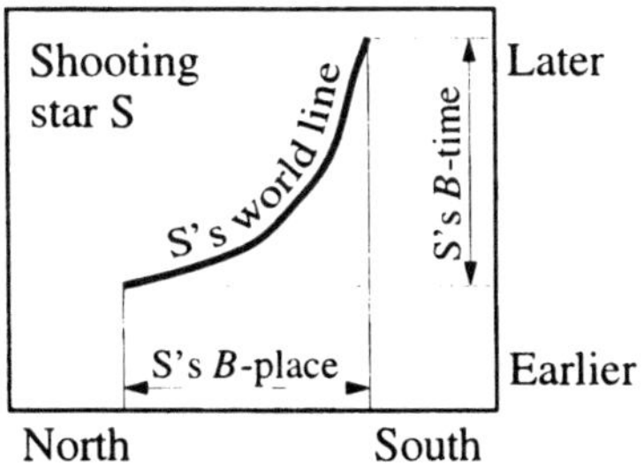

Figure 2

which gives all his locations in both space and time. The *B*-place of a thing or event suppresses most of the information in its world line by projecting the whole line onto the earth's surface, just as its *B*-time projects the line onto the dimension of time (as shown above in Figure 2 for a short-lived shooting star falling from north to south).

Usually, therefore, it is only worth giving the *B*-place of something whose world line is nearly parallel to the time axis, so that its spatial projection is not much larger than it is. In other words, only to things that do not move much, like hills, rivers and towns, do we normally bother to ascribe *B*-places. This is what makes them worth putting on a map: whenever we use the map to find them, they will always be where it shows them to be. People and other mobile things are not worth putting on maps, not because they have no *B*-places, but because their *B*-places are far larger than they are.

Calling *B*-places 'fixed' does not therefore mean that things do not move. It means only what I meant in chapter 1.3 by saying that *B*-times are fixed, i.e. that they do not vary over time; and for the same reason *B*-places do not vary across space. The latitude of Cambridge (52° north) is *everywhere* the same, just as the date of Hume's death (1776) is *always* the same. (Even those who think that 'Hume dies in year *n*' is true for no *n* until he dies do not think it could be true for one *n* now and for another *n* later, any more than 'Cambridge is *n*° north' could be true for one *n* here and for another *n* elsewhere.)

It follows that the *B*-places of things and events say nothing about how near or far they are from *here*, which is the spatial analogue of *now*. What tell us that are their *A*-places, the spatial analogues of *A*-times. *A*-places are linked by the same spatial relations that link *B*-places, just as *A*- and *B*-times are linked by the same temporal relations. Just as the same earlier–later relation links *1 June* with *2 June*, and *today* with *tomorrow*, so the same south–north relation links *52° north* with *53° north*, and *here* with *1° north of here*.

From this it follows that, just as one event's being a day later than another means it is always a day more future (or less past), so a thing *a*'s being 1° north of a thing *b* means that, wherever *here* may be, *a* is 1° more north (or less south) of here than *b* is. The latitude of *here* fixes the latitude of all *A*-places south and north of here, just as the *B*-time of the present fixes the *B*-times of all past and future *A*-times. In all these ways the array of *A*-places south and north (or east and west) of here is exactly analogous to the array of *A*-times earlier and later than now.

The analogy between places and times is of course imperfect. The earth's shape, as well as the greater dimensionality of space, makes my *A*- and *B*-places differ in structure from *A*- and *B*-times. Thus, while there may be no last moment of time, nowhere on earth is north of here at the north pole. Again, going west from here takes us to places that are also east of here, whereas the future does not turn into the past. And there is no spatial analogue of the fact that we can now see only what is past and affect only what is future. Nothing that important turns on whether something is north or south (or west or east) of here – which is why it does not matter which way we draw the analogy, i.e. whether we take south–north or north–south (or east–west or west–east) to correspond to earlier–later.

These differences do not however vitiate the analogies I have drawn, since I am not after all trying to show that time and space are alike. On the contrary, that is the inference I am resisting. But first it must be given a run for its money. And the earth's array of places is certainly analogous to the array of times in all the respects that matter here.

3 The *B*-theory of *A*-space

In particular, *A*-places vary across space just as *A*-times vary over time. Thus although here in Cambridge London is sixty miles south of here, that is not London's *A*-place everywhere. Forty miles north of here, London is a hundred miles away to the south; and eighty miles west of here, it is a hundred miles away to the south-east. While in London itself, sixty miles south of here, London is here and Cambridge is sixty miles away to the north. The *A*-places of London, Cambridge and everywhere else vary from place to place, just as the *A*-times of events vary from time to time.

So, besides all the fixed *B*-facts about distances and directions between *B*-places, there seem to be spatially variable *A*-facts about how far, and which way, *B*-places are from here. But we can explain these *A*-facts away, just as in chapter 3 we explained away their temporal counterparts. And as the explanation should now be obvious – and in the spatial case is not disputed – I shall simply sketch it, leaving readers to add the details.

The first step, as with time, is to trade in *A*-facts for *A*-truths. Then all we need for our spatial *A*-truths are spatial *B*-truthmakers, which are easily found. Take the proposition 'London is sixty miles south' and its tokens, e.g. signposts that say 'London 60' and point south. We know they are true sixty miles north of London and false everywhere else, and the reason is obvious. The *B*-fact that a *B*-place is sixty miles north of London is what makes this spatial *A*-proposition and its tokens true at that place: that is its spatial *B*-truthmaker there. And similarly for all other spatial *A*-propositions. They and their tokens are all made true at any *B*-place by spatial *B*-facts about that place. No spatial *A*-fact is needed to give any spatial *A*-proposition its truth value anywhere, and no one thinks it is.

This I believe is why there is no spatial analogue of tense logic. There easily could be, since *A*-place ascriptions are as iterable as *A*-time ones, as in 'Eighty miles west of here, London is a hundred miles away south-east'. Indeed the three dimensions of space generate *A*-entailments for a spatial *A*-logic that are far more complex than the *A*-entailments of its temporal counterpart. Yet despite its fascinating formal potential, no one has yet developed such a logic, and I doubt if anyone will, since no one believes in the spatial *A*-facts it would claim to relate.

Nor is anyone impressed by the fact that all our experiences happen to us here, wherever here may be. This is the spatial analogue of the presence of experience and, like it, is the basis of our knowledge of other *A*-truths. It is only because I know my experiences to be both *here* and *in Cambridge* that I know Cambridge is here, that London is sixty miles from here, etc. But why then, when so many are impressed by the *temporal* presence of experience, is no one impressed by its *spatial* presence? The answer, I am sure, is that no one thinks the latter to be more than a trivial tautology. Because my experiences are wherever I am, my belief that they are here must be made true by the fact that this token belief is where they are.

In short, despite there being spatial analogues of everything that leads many people to believe in temporal *A*-facts, no one believes in spatial *A*-facts. No one thinks that Cambridge, as well as being 52° north and 0° east, sixty miles north of London, etc., also has the spatially variable property of being *here*. Whatever their views on time, all parties agree that things and events in space are – literally – neither here nor there.

4 The difference between time and space

In chapters 3 and 4, I gave the temporal analogue of this universally accepted account of spatial *A*-truths, and will use it later to show that just as nothing is in reality *here* or *there*, so nothing is in reality *now* or *then*. In this respect I shall indeed treat time like space, and for exactly analogous reasons, i.e. for reasons which, if they apply to either case, apply to both.

As these reasons are moreover the key reasons for denying *A*-facts, those who reject them to save temporal *A*-facts cannot easily explain why, as we all agree, there are no spatial *A*-facts. Space and time can therefore only differ in this respect if the difference is too basic to be explained, and this is what most advocates of temporal *A*-facts believe. For them, what makes time differ from the dimensions of space is precisely that while there are temporal *A*-facts there are no spatial ones. They think that if there were in reality no past, present or future, there would be no real difference between what we call time and the other dimensions of an unchanging spacetime.

But this is not true. No *A*-facts are needed to make temporal relations observably different from all spatial ones. Take the example in chapter 1.5 of my seeing that a clock's second hand is moving clockwise. I do this by distinguishing a temporal and a spatial relation, both of which I can see hold between two events: namely, the hand's passing the figure '1' both *earlier than* and *to the left of* its passing the figure '2'. And as I argued in chapter 1.4, I need see no *A*-facts to see this. I may indeed assume that the events I see are nearby and so only recently past; but they need not be, and they do not look to be. I might be looking through a telescope at events long past and far away, or even precognising events in the future: either way the events would still *look* the same.

In short, I need not see any spatial or temporal *A*-facts in order to see how my clock hand moves, and hence to see that one event is earlier than and to the left of another. So I can easily deny the existence of any such *A*-facts without denying our obvious ability to see and distinguish the spatial and temporal relations which define the *B*-places and *B*-times of things and events.

Nor does denying the existence of *A*-facts require me to deny either the fact of change or its temporal nature. The movement of a clock's second hand is a case of change, and I can see it as such without seeing or assuming any *A*-facts. For if I can distinguish temporal from spatial relations, I can certainly distinguish change in a clock hand's position from, say, a spatial variation in its width from one end of it to the other.

We *B*-theorists still need to show of course why variation over time is change when variation across space is not; but we need no *A*-facts to show that, as I shall prove in chapter 8 by showing it without them. And in so doing I shall show why we *B*-theorists need not deny this (or any other) real difference between time and space. Those who insist that time differs

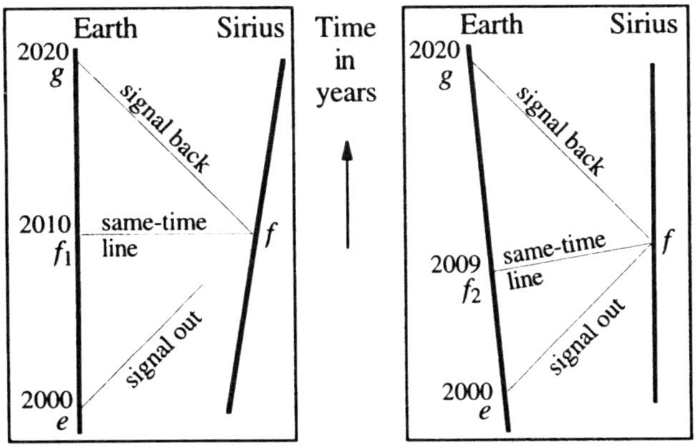

Earth frame Distance in light years Sirian frame

Figure 3

from space, and that temporal change exists, need not part company with us on that account.

5 Relativity

Nor need they part company with Einstein's theories of relativity. Contrary to some early misreadings, his special and general theories do not deny that time differs from space. They do indeed give time and space a single measure, and a four-dimensional geometry, which Newtonian spacetime lacks. They also let spacetime distances be divided in more ways than one into spatial and temporal components, and this is what provoked the widespread suspicion that they confounded the two. And while that suspicion is less widespread now, it may still be common enough to justify one more attempt to dispel it. And for that we need only consider the simpler special theory. The complications of general relativity will not make time any more like space than the special theory does.

Look then at Figure 3, a variant of Figure 1 from chapter 1.4. It shows a light signal sent (*e*) from the earth at the first moment of the new millennium and reflected from Sirius (*f*) back to earth (*g*). As before, suppose Sirius is ten light years off, so that the *B*-time of *g*, the signal's return to earth, is the start of 2020. What is the date of *f*, the signal's reflection from Sirius, i.e. the *B*-time of an earthly event that is simultaneous with *f*? The natural answer, shown in the earth frame of Figure 3, is that *f* is simultaneous with an event f_1 which occurs at the start of 2010; and if the earth really were at rest, as its rest frame takes it to be, that would be so.

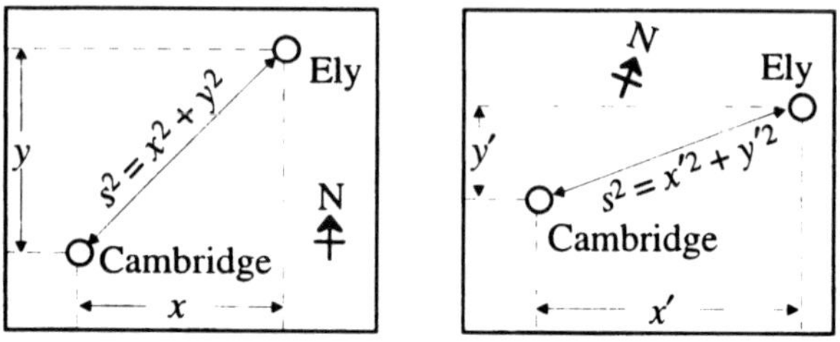

Figure 4

But special relativity, like classical mechanics, provides no means of distinguishing rest from motion at a constant velocity. And unlike classical mechanics, it makes different earthly velocities give *e* quite different dates. Thus as Figure 3 shows, if we were moving rapidly away from a stationary Sirius, *f* might be simultaneous in Sirius's rest frame with an earthly event f_2 in 2009. Other frames would give *f* even earlier, or later, dates, ranging from just after the start of 2000 to just before the start of 2020. So if, as special relativity implies, nothing in reality makes one frame right and others wrong, nothing fixes *f*'s temporal distance from earthly events such as e, f_1, f_2 and *g* to within twenty years.

Moreover, as the temporal distance *t* between *f* and f_1 (say) varies from frame to frame, so does their spatial distance *s*, in such a way as to keep the same value, in any frame, of a function *d* given by

(1) $d^2 = s^2 - (ct)^2$,

where *c* is the speed of light in a vacuum and the same in all frames. *d* is *f*'s and f_1's so-called *spacetime separation*, and its constancy across frames means that, within limits, their spatial and temporal distances are interchangeable. In this respect it makes those distances like the coordinates of the spatial separation *s* between, say, Cambridge and Ely, which we can also give in different spatial reference frames, as shown above in Figure 4.

In Figure 4, the axes of frame A run, as usual, north–south and east–west, while those of frame B are rotated about 20° clockwise. This makes *s*'s coordinates vary from frame to frame, being *x* and *y* in A and *x*′ and *y*′ in B, while *s* itself, the function given in any frame by

(2) $s^2 = x^2 + y^2 = x'^2 + y'^2 = \ldots$,

is a constant, as *d* is in (1). The reason is obvious: the function *s*, the direct distance between Cambridge and Ely, is their only real spatial separation.

The coordinates of s, like the north–south x and the east–west y, are merely projections of s onto arbitrarily chosen spatial directions.

Similarly, one might conclude for f and f_1, with the function d. This, the direct spacetime distance between f and f_1, is their only real spacetime separation. d's coordinates s and t are just projections of d onto arbitrarily chosen spacetime directions. But then does it not follow that temporal directions in relativistic spacetime can no more differ in kind from spatial directions than the latter can differ from each other? Must not the earlier–later direction of any relativistic reference frame be just like its north–south, east–west and up–down directions?

No. Relativity does indeed allow us a striking latitude in our dating of celestial events, with a compensating latitude in their spatial distance from us. But this does not make time in relativity at all like space. For a start, relativity treats temporal and spatial distances quite differently, as we can see by expanding (1) into

(3) $d^2 = x^2+y^2+z^2-(ct)^2$,

which clearly distinguishes t from x, y and z, the three coordinates of s. Furthermore t and s are of course measured quite differently, t by clocks and s by rangefinders. This fact alone – which is what makes t the temporal distance and s the spatial one – is enough to show that t and s differ in kind.

Thus, far from denying a distinction of kind between t and s, relativity presupposes one. The link it imposes on Δt and Δs, the differences in their values between any two frames, namely that

(4) $\Delta s = c\Delta t$,

is an exchange rate, not an identity.

Finally, relativity draws an absolute distinction between so-called *spacelike* and *timelike* separations of pairs of events. The former are separations for which d^2 is positive, which entails that in no frame are the separated events in the same place, even though in some they are simultaneous. For in any frame where s=0, d^2=–$(ct)^2$; and this, as $(ct)^2$ cannot be negative, makes d^2 negative, which by hypothesis it is not. So for all pairs of events whose d^2 is positive, their being separated in space, if not their exact spatial distance, is an absolute fact, independent of our choice of reference frame, as their time order is not. Hence the name 'spacelike' for their separation.

Similarly for *timelike* separations, those for which d^2 is negative, which entails that in no frame are the separated events simultaneous, although in some they are in the same place. For in any frame where t=0, d^2=s^2; and this, as s^2 cannot be negative, makes d^2 positive, which by hypothesis it is not. Thus all pairs of events for which d^2 is negative are separated in time, and have indeed the same time order, in all frames. So their time order, if not their exact temporal distance, is an absolute fact, independent of our choice of reference frame, as their spatial separation is not. Hence the name 'timelike' for their separation.

What of pairs of events for which $d^2=0$? (1) tells us that in this case $s=ct$, so that if $t\neq 0$, $s/t=c$, the speed of light. So for events linked by light, as *e* and *f* are in Figure 3, *d* is zero. In this case, therefore, 'separation' is a misleading name for *d*, since it suggests that events with 'zero separation' are not really separated in spacetime, which of course *e* and *f* are. They also have an absolute time order, for since even light must leave before it can arrive, *e* precedes *f* in all reference frames. For this reason I propose to call the separation of these events too 'timelike'.

To sum up: relativity not only measures and treats temporal and spatial distances differently, it also gives many events and hence places in spacetime an absolute temporal order, just as it gives others an absolute spatial separation. In short, relativity does nothing to conflate time with space, and no one should be led to reject – or accept – it by thinking that it does. But nor does it vitiate any of the distinctions and analogies between time and space drawn earlier in this chapter. This being so, we can simplify the ensuing argument by ignoring it.

6 Relativity and the present

But not before noting the serious problem which relativity poses for *A*-theorists, by preventing their distinctions between past, present and future bearing the factual loads that motivate them. Take the presentist view, that only the present exists. On this view the only events on Sirius which now exist are those that are simultaneous with your present reading of this very sentence. Yet in relativity, as we have seen, if Sirius is ten light years away, which events these are will vary from frame to frame over a twenty-year span. And if nothing in the world makes one frame right, nothing will ever make any shortlived Sirian event present as opposed to past or future. It will be present in some frames, past in some and future in some, and that is all there is to it. But that can hardly be all there is to existence.

This is not only a problem for presentists. Those who think that the past and present exist, but the future does not, so that to become present is to come into existence, face it too. So do those who, while they reject *A*-facts, think that not even *B*-facts about events exist until they do. On these views also the existence of events depends on their simultaneity, either with what is present here or with each other. So for these views too the existence of remote events can be a matter of fact at any earthly time *t* only if their simultaneity with events here at *t* is also a matter of fact, which in relativity it is not.

In short, adding relativity to any of these views makes existence relative to places as well as times, which is incredible. The truth of a statement that Einstein exists may depend on *when* it is made; it can hardly depend also on *where* it is made. This is why *A*-theorists would like modern physics, and especially modern cosmology, to provide a single right reference frame, in order to make simultaneity a matter of fact across the whole of space. And as some think modern cosmology has done this, I should say briefly why I think it has not.

The expansion of the universe takes remote galaxies away from us at speeds, proportional to their distances, given by the so-called Hubble constant (about 0.037 m/sec per light year). We can use this fact to define unique local reference frames in which the Hubble constant is the same in all directions. (This in turn defines local velocities, like that of the earth, by how much and in which directions they make the Hubble constant vary.) And we may grant that, since the universe is expanding uniformly, such frames exist everywhere. Will they do what *A*-theorists want?

Obviously not. For as the universe *is* expanding, anything at rest in any one such frame will be moving in every other. Thus in the rest frame of a galaxy G, *n* light years north of us, anything at rest in our frame will be moving south at 0.037*n* metres per second. But this is just Figure 3 writ large, with G replacing Sirius: at any earthly date, our frame and G's will make different G-events present. And as the uniformity taken for granted by modern cosmology stops anything making any one of these frames right and the others wrong, this is bad news for *A*-theorists. Cosmology, far from saving them from special relativity, only makes matters worse.

Whereas to those of us *B*-theorists who deny that spacewide distinctions of past, present and future are factual, it matters not a whit that they can be drawn in many ways, all equally true to all the facts there are. The fact, noted in chapter 1.4, that different reference frames generate different *A* and *B* series poses no problem for us.

However, although I see no way of reconciling *A*-theories of time with our spacetime physics, I shall not press that point here, for two reasons. One is that *A*-theorists may, and some do, use this incompatibility to reject that physics – a healthy (if rash) reaction when so many philosophers are absurdly credulous of the wildest speculations of physicists about time. But my main reason for not pressing the objection is that I do not need to. *A*-theories of time face even stronger objections, as we shall see in chapter 7. The support that relativity and modern cosmology give to the *B*-theory of time, although very welcome, is by no means necessary.

6 *Thinking in time*

1 The irreducibility of *A*-beliefs

So much for the canard that *B*-time is spacelike. I shall say more later about how time differs from space, apropos of change and causation. Until then I shall take the difference for granted, and I must not be thought to spatialise time when I invoke its spatial analogues, as I must do now to discredit two more invalid inferences from *B*-theories of time: namely, that they require *A*-beliefs to be reducible to, or replaceable by, *B*-beliefs.

The conclusions of both these inferences are as obviously false of space as of time. It is equally obvious that belief in here- and now-propositions, like 'Cambridge is here' and 'It is now AD 2000', cannot be reduced to or replaced by *B*-beliefs. But whereas this makes no one adopt *A*-theories of space, it does encourage *A*-theories of time. So the spatial inferences must to start with be more obviously discreditable. Yet the temporal inferences are only valid if the spatial ones are. So it should help to discredit them if we look at space and time together, starting with the first inference.

Why then might *B*-theories of space and time be thought to entail that *A*-beliefs about them reduce to *B*-beliefs? One train of thought runs as follows. Suppose that, as we *B*-theorists claim, *B*-facts are what make all *A*-propositions true where and when they are true. They are what make 'Cambridge is here' true in and only in Cambridge, 'It is now AD 2000' true in and only in AD 2000, and so on. The *B*-truthmakers of all *A*-propositions are what fix the *B*-conditions in which they, and thus sentences expressing them, are true.

Note next that the meanings of many sentences look very much like their truth conditions. Consider '*x* is half empty'. The truth condition of this sentence, for any *x*, is that *x* is half full, a fact that makes the sentence synonymous with '*x* is half full'. Which is why, pub lore notwithstanding, believing a glass to be half empty is the same as believing it to be half full.

Now apply these ideas to our *A*-sentences, abbreviating 'Cambridge' to 'C' and our millennial date to 'M'. Then for any *B*-place *s*, 'C is here' is true at *s* if and only if *s* is where C is; and for any *B*-time *t*, 'It is now M' is true at *t* if and only if *t* is in (or is) M. Those are the *B*-truth-conditions of these *A*-sentences. So those are their meanings. So to believe them is to believe the sentences which state those meanings. But those sentences are *B*-sentences:

'"C is here" is true at and only at C'

(to abridge somewhat) is true everywhere; and (as we noted in chapter 4.1)

'"It is now M" is true at and only at M'

is true always. So must not the *A*-beliefs that C is here and that it is now M reduce to the *B*-beliefs these sentences express?

I hope not, since this apparent consequence of the *B*-theory seems to me clearly false. We cannot identify these *A*-sentences' *B*-truth-conditions with their meanings, since the former vary across space and time, and the latter I think do not. Yet some philosophers think they do, which is why I said in chapter 3.1 that we might take the *A*-sentence 'Jim races tomorrow' to express a new *B*-proposition every day: on 1 June, that he races on 2 June; on 2 June, that he races on 3 June; and so on. But these propositions are this sentence's *B*-truth-conditions. So if they are what this *A*-sentence means, my *A*-belief in it will reduce to a sequence of *B*-beliefs: on 1 June, that Jim races on 2 June; on 2 June, that he races on 3 June; and so on.

I have three objections to this reduction. First, it implies that what I believe when I believe 'Jim races tomorrow' changes every day, and that to know what this belief is I must know what day it is (i.e. which *B*-day is today). A theory with these implications compares very badly with an *A*-theory which says that what I believe – that Jim races tomorrow – is the same every day, and therefore that I can know what this belief is without knowing what day it is. Second, as I said in chapter 3.1, taking *A*-sentences to express *B*-propositions begs the question against *A*-theorists. And third, an *A*-sentence must surely, as *A*-theorists say, have *some* constant meaning which we need not know the time to know. So I reckon we *B*-theorists must also give *A*-sentences constant meanings, and these cannot be their variable *B*-truth-conditions.

They can however be *functions*, from *B*-places and *B*-times to the *B*-truth-conditions of *A*-sentences at those places and times, which I shall call 'truth-condition functions' or, for short, 'tc-functions'. This makes 'C is here' mean the tc-function from any *B*-place *s* to *s*'s being where C is, and 'It is now M' mean the tc-function from any *B*-time *t* to *t*'s being in (or being) M.

Similarly for other indexical sentences, including those that in chapter 3.3 I called 'personal' – like 'Jim races *me*', which means the tc-function from any person *x* to Jim's racing *x*. Similarly even for *B*-sentences, whose meanings we may also equate with functions from places, times and people to their *B*-truth-conditions at those spatial, temporal and personal locations. Only the tc-functions of *B*-sentences are what are called *constant* functions, i.e. they have the same values (*B*-truth-conditions) for all their arguments (places, times and people). This gives us a single *B*-theory of the meanings of both *A*- and *B*-sentences.

The idea that sentences mean tc-functions prompts several sceptical questions. What is it, for example, to believe such a function? Well, what is it to believe the truth condition that many philosophers say is what a *B*-sentence like 'Jim races Jack' means? Obviously, it is to believe that this truth condition obtains, i.e. that Jim does in fact race Jack. This being so, to believe a tc-function must be to believe that whatever truth condition is its value for the relevant arguments (place, time, person) obtains. But how do believers know which the relevant arguments are, and hence which the relevant truth conditions are? The answer is that they may not, and need not, know this, since a tc-function's arguments for any person at any place and time can be that very person, place and time whether he or she knows it or not.

(It is indeed a good question how our beliefs manage to refer to us, and to when and where we are, when we do not know who, when or where we are; but this is not a question I need go into here, since all that matters here is that our beliefs can, and do, do this. For one answer to the question, however, see my 'I and Now', 1989.)

A more positive argument for taking sentences to mean tc-functions is this. It is fairly obvious that, in order to understand an *A*- or *B*-sentence when we hear it, and to be able to use it properly ourselves, all we need to know is what its truth conditions are for any person at any place and time. (I take using a sentence properly to include not asserting it or its negation when we cannot tell if it is true or false because we cannot tell whether its truth conditions obtain.) And it is still more obvious that to understand and to be able to use a sentence properly is to know what it means. But if so, then to know that, for any *B*-place *s* and *B*-time *t*, '*s* is here' is true at and only at *s*, and 'It is now *t*' is true at and only at *t*, is to know what '... is here' and 'It is now ...' mean.

This moreover, as I have just noted, is knowledge that does not require us to know in any particular case what *s* or *t* is. For we can know what any function (like $x+y$) is without knowing what its arguments (e.g. $x=2$, $y=5$) happen on any occasion to be. So if 'Jim races tomorrow' means the tc-function from any *B*-day *d* to Jim's racing on day $d+1$, then I can know what this *A*-sentence means, and hence what I believe by believing it, whether or not I know which day *d* is.

So far so good for our tc-functions. But then, as in our 'half full = half empty' case, should not the *B*-sentences which state the tc-functions of 'C is here' and 'It is now M' mean what those *A*-sentences mean? Yet clearly they do not, since, as we have just seen, their own truth conditions, unlike the truth conditions they state, do *not* vary across space or time. That is what makes it impossible for these or any other *B*-sentences to translate 'C is here' or 'It is now M', and hence for these, or any other, *A*-beliefs to be reduced to any *B*-belief.

Yet why, now we have given 'C is here' and 'It is now M' invariant *B*-meanings, should the invariance of a *B*-sentence's *B*-truth-condition stop it meaning what these *A*-sentences mean? It is obvious that it does, but less obvious why. Perhaps it is because the meanings of indexical sentences cannot really be identified with tc-functions? The whole idea of equating meanings with truth conditions is after all debatable, and it is especially debatable whether meanings supervene on truth conditions, i.e. whether having the same truth conditions entails having the same meaning.

But the reason we cannot translate *A*-sentences by *B*-sentences is not that their meanings differ from tc-functions. On the contrary, what makes them untranslatable is the very fact that their meanings do entail these functions. And this entailment, unlike its converse, is not at all debatable. For even if meanings need not supervene on truth conditions, truth conditions must surely supervene on meanings: two sentences cannot be synonymous if they are true in quite different conditions. And an *A*-sentence whose truth conditions vary across space or time is bound to be true in quite different conditions from any *B*-sentence, whose truth conditions do not vary in that way. This is the real reason why no *B*-sentence can translate 'C is here', 'It is now M' or any other contingent *A*-sentence.

For readers who, perhaps because they are reluctant to relate meanings to truth conditions at all, are still unpersuaded, I have another argument. As *B*-sentences, if true at all, are nowhere and never false, their being true at a given *B*-location does nothing to identify that location. Thus, as I noted in chapter 4.1, tokens of '"It is now *t*" is true at *t*' say nothing about *when* they occur; and similarly, tokens of '"*s* is here" is true at *s*' say nothing about *where* they occur. This is why these *B*-sentences are useless for telling people where they are or what the time is. Yet those are the most frequent uses of tokens of '*s* is here' and 'It is now *t*': it is why clocks emit the latter and train station announcers emit the former.

This surely settles the matter. For however we relate meanings to truth conditions, no modern analytic philosopher will risk excommunication by denying that meanings must be closely related to use. And however loosely we apply that doctrine, we could not take two sentences to be synonymous if, as here, they cannot be used in anything like the same way. No theory of meaning as use can let any *B*-sentences mean what either *A*-theorists or I take '*s* is here' and 'It is now *t*' to mean. And if, as all agree, this fact is no evidence for spatial *A*-facts, it can hardly be evidence for temporal *A*-facts either.

2 *A*-meanings and *B*-truth-conditions

Some however may still be tempted to suppose that, if *A*-sentences cannot be translated by *B*-sentences, we do after all need *A*-facts, like the fact that C is here, or that it is now M, to be their meanings. How should that temptation be resisted?

First, by resisting a bad analogy. Sometimes, as in mathematics, there must indeed be more to meaning than truth conditions. For as mathematical truths are all necessarily true, each is true in the same conditions, namely in all conditions. So '2+2=4' is true if and only if there is no greatest prime number. But '2+2=4' does not *mean* there is no greatest prime number. Someone who already understands '2+2=4' will not learn what 'There is no greatest prime number' means by learning that they have the same truth conditions.

But our contingent *A*-sentences are not like this. As I argued in §1, the fact that they do not *mean* the same as the *B*-sentences which state their tc-functions does not stop those sentences *giving* their meanings. To know that, for any *B*-place *s* and *B*-time *t*, '*s* is here' is true at and only at *s* and 'It is now *t*' is true at and only at *t*, *is* to know just what those sentences mean. Given just this knowledge, we can produce and understand tokens of these *A*-sentences anywhere and at any time, and distinguish them from tokens of any other *A*-sentences whose different tc-functions we also know.

(We must admittedly also be able to recognise what I have called the 'presence of experience', in order to know that we are perceiving a token of 'It is now *t*' *now* or a token of '*s* is here' *here*. But I have already given a *B*-theory of the temporal presence of experience in chapter 4, and sketched its obvious spatial analogue at the end of chapter 5.3.)

I believe therefore that our use of contingent *A*-sentences, unlike that of mathematical sentences, can be completely explained by our knowledge of how the truth of what we say depends on where and when we say it. In particular, the *different* meanings of different *A*-sentences can be distinguished, as those of mathematical sentences cannot, by their different tc-functions. 'C is here' and 'C is sixty miles away', for example, are used differently because they are known to be true in different places, just as 'It is now M' and 'M is two years hence' are used differently because they are known to be true at different times.

Truth conditions give meanings less debatably here than in mathematics and elsewhere for another reason too. For a sentence's truth conditions to give its meaning, its being true in them must be more than a coincidence. Otherwise 'Snow is white' could mean that grass is green. For since 'Snow is white' *is* true and grass *is* green, 'Snow is white' is indeed true if and only if grass is green. But that of course is just a coincidence. Even if grass was not green, 'Snow is white' would still be true – *if* snow was still white. So for the truth conditions of 'Snow is white' to rule out this and all other misreadings of it, they must include not only actual but all possible conditions. We must take 'Snow is white' to be true in all possible worlds where snow is white and false in all others.

To give meanings, therefore, truth conditions must include imaginary as well as actual conditions. But how much can truth in imaginary conditions tell us about actual meanings? Even if we could travel to imaginary worlds, we could still not check the meaning of 'Snow is white' by going to worlds where, say, snow is white and grass is not green, and seeing that 'Snow is white' (as used in our world) is still true there. It is the other way round: what tells us that 'Snow is white' is true in such a world is that we use this sentence to mean that snow is white.

If this is an objection to using truth conditions to give meanings, it does not apply to *A*-sentences. For we *can* check what '... is here' means by seeing that, for any actual *s*, '*s* is here' is always taken to be true at and only at *s*; and similarly for 'It is now *t*'. To give the spatial and temporal meanings of contingent *A*-sentences, we need only say where and when they would be true in our world. In these cases tc-functions seem to me to give meanings in a way that is both innocuous and effective.

There is moreover nothing about the meanings of *A*-sentences that *A*-facts could tell us which *B*-facts cannot. For the only aspect of a sentence's meaning which facts of either kind can supply is its truth conditions, that after all being what they are defined to do. All that the supposed *A*-facts, that C is here and that it is now M, can do for 'C is here' and 'It is now M' is to make them true where and when these facts exist. They can do nothing to make these sentences important or poetic or memorable: merely true. But as we have now seen, that job can be done equally well by *B*-facts. So if doing that job fails to give the meanings of *A*-sentences, the lacuna will not be filled by *A*-facts.

In any case, as we have seen, there is no such lacuna to fill. The way in which *B*-facts make an *A*-sentence true where and when it is true *does* give its meaning, and does so in a way which explains immediately why no *B*-sentence can translate it. On our *B*-theory this follows at once from the fact that the tc-functions of *B*-sentences are constant and those of *A*-sentences are not. That, I say, is what makes *A*-beliefs irreducible to *B*-beliefs.

3 Actions and beliefs

If we *B*-theorists can say why *A*-beliefs are irreducible, can we also say why they are indispensable? It is not at once obvious that we can, since it is not obvious why, if there are no *A*-facts, we must think and speak as if there were. Yet we obviously need to know more about the locations of people, things and events in space and time than their *B*-locations. To inform our interactions with them we must also know which of them we are faced with, i.e. which of them are spatially and temporally present. But then if, like patriotism, knowledge of *B*-facts is not enough, must there not also be *A*-facts that we need to know? Is this not why we need true *A*-beliefs?

That does not follow. The existence of *A*-facts need not be what makes us need true *A*-beliefs. We may need true *A*-beliefs simply because we need beliefs which, while true, are not true everywhere and always. But why should *B*-theorists think this? One answer they can give is that we need *A*-beliefs because we are *agents*, most if not all of whose actions depend on what we believe, and depend for their success on when they are done. This, as I shall now show, requires us to have *A*-beliefs, even in a world devoid of *A*-facts.

First, it is obvious, and not seriously disputed, that most if not all of our actions are caused (usually via our intentions) by our beliefs and desires. There may indeed be some actions which we do entirely for their own sakes and which we can do without thinking how to do them: the causes of those actions may well not include any beliefs about how to do what we want to do. But most actions are not like this, being done at least partly in order to do something else, as when I go out in order to shop, take a coat to keep warm, cook food to eat, and so on. All these actions are caused not only by what I want but also by something I believe: that the shops are open, that it is cold out, that the food I am cooking is edible, and so on.

Suppose, for example, I turn on the radio to hear the six o'clock news. I do this because I want to hear the news and believe it starts at six. That is why I turn the radio on. But why do I turn it on *at six*? Not just because I want to hear the news at six, since I may have wanted to do that all day. Not even because I believe the news starts at six: that belief too I could have had all day. Something more is needed to make me act when I do, and it is obvious what it is: I need to believe that it is six *now*. Until I acquire this *A*-belief I shall do nothing, however much I want to hear the news, and however strong my *B*-belief that it is on at six. But if I *do* have that desire and that *B*-belief, then my coming to believe at six that it is now six will cause me to act at six. (Or as soon afterwards as makes no odds: here, as in chapter 4.4, we may ignore the time it takes me to acquire and act on my beliefs.)

Notice next that the relevant cause of this action is an *A-belief*, not an *A-fact*. For suppose there are such facts, including the fact that it is now six, a fact which exists only at six. So if this fact did cause my action, it would indeed explain why I act at six and not earlier or later, when the fact does not exist. But that in itself is enough to show that this fact cannot be what causes my action, since if it was I *could* not act earlier or later, which of course I could. I could easily turn on the radio before or after six; and so I will, if it is before or after six that I come to believe (falsely) that it is now six. In short, what causes me to act at any *B*-time *t* cannot be that at *t* it *is* now six; it must be that at *t* I *believe* it is now six. It is my *A*-belief, not the *A*-fact, that makes me turn my radio on when I do; and it will do so whether or not it is true, i.e. whether or not the *A*-fact exists.

As in this case, so in general. It is our beliefs that make us act as and when we do, not the *A*- or *B*-facts which make those beliefs true. And given our desires, surroundings and abilities, our beliefs will make us act in the same way whether they are true or false. If I want to hear the six o'clock news, have a radio that works (and that I can work) and no conflicting desires, I will turn the radio on when I believe it is now six, whether it is or not. The truth value of this *A*-belief of mine is irrelevant to how it makes me act.

What it *is* relevant to is whether my action succeeds. Only if my belief that it is now six is true, i.e. only at six, will the action it causes succeed, i.e. succeed in getting me what I want, which is to hear the start of the six o'clock news.

Again, as in this case, so in general. Truth is the property of our beliefs which ensures the success of any actions they combine with our desires to cause, i.e. which ensures that those actions will achieve what we do them to achieve. If, as I believe, the shops are open when I go out to shop, I will get to shop, and if not, not. If, as I believe, it is cold out, the coat I put on to keep me warm will do so, and if not, not (since I would be warm in any case). If and only if, as I believe, the food I am cooking is edible will it feed me. And so on.

This thesis about truth needs developing, of course, e.g. to cover actions caused by many beliefs, or by very weak ones (as when a minute degree of belief that I will win the lottery if I buy a ticket causes me to do so). It also faces apparent counter-examples, as when the falsity of beliefs that we act on cancels out: I am late turning on the radio, but so is the news, so my action succeeds anyway. These challenges and objections can all be met (see Whyte 1990), but I need not try to meet them here. All I need here is the undeniable fact that, generally if not always, the truth conditions of beliefs are, as a matter of fact, those in which the actions they cause succeed.

This is all it takes to explain in *B*-terms why agents need *A*-beliefs. For as my examples show, the success of most if not all of our actions depends on when and where they are done. The news is not always on, shop hours vary from place to place, it is colder out at night (and near the poles), food goes off faster when and where it is hot, and so on. So for our actions to succeed they need to be caused by beliefs which are true when and where we have them, but are not true always and everywhere.

This is what makes all agents need true beliefs with *B*-truth-conditions that vary over time and space. Without them we could not time or place the myriad actions which, if they are to get us what we want, must be done at the right *B*-time and right *B*-place. True *B*-beliefs alone, precisely because they are true always and everywhere, cannot tell us when or where to act. That is why, even in worlds without *A*-facts, agents will still need *A*-beliefs to enable them to take timely action. Our obvious need of such beliefs is thus no evidence that ours is no such world.

4 Experiencing the flow of time

To be capable of timely action it is not of course enough to have *A*-beliefs: we must have them only when they are true. (And also *where* they are true, but this we may take as read, since our beliefs are always where we are.) And so on the whole we do. We make mistakes, naturally: not all our *A*-beliefs are true, any more than all our *B*-beliefs are; but many are. But as *A*-propositions, unlike *B*-propositions, change their truth values from time to time, if we are to keep our *A*-beliefs true we must keep changing them, and some more often than others. My *A*-beliefs about the day of Jim's race need changing only once a day, from 'Jim races two days hence' to 'Jim races tomorrow' to 'Jim races today' to 'Jim raced yesterday', and so on. How often my now-beliefs about the time need changing depends on how precise they are: once a year if they tell me what year it is; every second during a countdown to the start of a race; and so on.

We have so many *A*-beliefs that we must always be changing some of them, especially our now-beliefs. These changes embody the psychological truth in the metaphysical falsehood that time flows, i.e. that events like Jim's race really are moving in *A*-time, from being tomorrow, to being today, to being yesterday, and so on. On a *B*-theory of course time does not flow, since there are no such *A*-facts as Jim's racing tomorrow, today and yesterday to come into and go out of existence. Yet even we *B*-theorists can admit, if not a real flow of time, then a real, and often true, experience of time flowing, as follows.

I said in §3 that I need two beliefs to make me turn on my radio to hear the six o'clock news: one, that the news starts at six; the other, that it is six now. This is not quite right. What makes me act is not that I *have* the belief that it is now six, but that I *get* this belief. This cause of my action is a *change* in an *A*-belief, from believing that six is future to believing that it is present.

So far I have ignored the difference between having a property at a time and gaining or losing it at a time, because so far such differences have not mattered. This is why in chapter 1.2 I decided for the time being to call 'all past, present or future entities, other than moments or intervals of time, "events"'. But here the difference between beliefs and changes in them does matter, since it is the latter, not the former, which embody our experience of the flow of time.

Not all changes of belief do this, however. For a start, experiences are conscious, and since most beliefs are rarely conscious, so too are most of their changes. For example, as I rarely call to mind my beliefs about shop hours, the daily change from my believing the shops are now open to believing they are now shut is rarely a conscious experience. But many, if not all, of the changes in the now-beliefs induced in me by my senses are conscious, and these will serve to show how we can truly experience a flow of time which does not in fact exist.

First however I must say more about how our senses change our *A*-beliefs. The changes needed to keep our *A*-beliefs true do not happen automatically. That is why we need clocks to tell us the time, and eyes and ears to tell us what our clocks are saying (and what else is happening as they say it). In telling us all this our senses change not only our now-beliefs but also our past- and future-beliefs. My seeing that a shop is now open tells me also that its opening is now past and that its closing again is now future; and so on. Most if not all changes in our past- and future-beliefs are caused, directly or indirectly, by changes in our now-beliefs caused by our senses.

But how can our senses give us new now-beliefs if, as I argued in chapter 1.5 and said again in chapter 5.4, we never see the *A*-times of events? How for example can my seeing a clock's display change from '5.59' to '6.00' tell me that it is now six if I cannot see that this change is happening *now*? The answer I gave in chapter 4.4 was that if I trust the clock, its saying '6.00' at any *B*-time *t* will cause me to believe at *t* that it is now six. So if the clock is right, and says '6.00' at six, this display will be true while it exists (i.e. until it changes to '6.01' at 6.01), and so will my now-belief, that it is six, which the clock will cause me to have until 6.01.

But how then do we learn to trust clocks, and to tell in general if what we see and hear is happening more or less as we see and hear it? This is undoubtedly our default assumption – or rather habit, since we need not infer, even unconsciously, that what we see is happening as we see it: our eyes need only habitually cause us to have now-beliefs rather than future- or past-beliefs. But where does this habit come from; and what makes us modify it, as we learn to do when we hear thunder or look at the stars?

The answer to the first question lies, I think, in evolution. What makes our default habit useful is that the light which shows us nearby events travels far faster than we can, or need to, react to them. This is true in particular of events, like the approach of predators, partners or food, on our timely reaction to which we and our species depend for survival. If we let our eyes give us future-beliefs about these events, we would not act on them in time; if we let them give us very past-beliefs, we would not act on them at all; and either way we would die out. It is only the habit of letting our eyes give us now-beliefs that lets us survive, which is why we are born with it, precisely because, when it matters, it almost always gives us *A*-beliefs only when they are true.

This is also why, and when, we modify this habit, namely when, and because, we find that it would *not* give us *A*-beliefs when they are true. What tells us this is the evidence for theories which entail it, such as those that tell us the speeds of light and sound, and the distances of the stars we see and the thunder we hear. These cases, however, are too infrequent and unimportant in practice to shake our default habit of believing events to happen more or less as we see them. So for present purposes too we can ignore them.

Let us then assume for simplicity that what we see happens more or less as we see it, so that our seeing it makes us believe truly that it is happening now. This will still not make all our *A*-beliefs true, for three reasons. First, our eyes may deceive us in other respects. When they tell me that Jim is racing now, they may be right about the time but wrong about the man: it may be Jim's twin brother Jack. Second, we rely for most of our past-beliefs on memory and testimony, both of which can be wrong not only about what happened but about when it happened. It may be three years ago, not two, as I now believe, that I was last in Australia; and Jim's sister Jane may be older than she says she is. Third, we may fail to change our *A*-beliefs when they become false because our senses fail to make us do so, as when I miss a meeting because I forget to keep my eye on the time.

Yet even if in practice we will certainly fail to keep *all* our *A*-beliefs true, we could succeed in principle. And if we did, then the changes in our *A*-beliefs would correspond exactly to the changes that *A*-theorists take to constitute the flow of time. They say that Jim's race changes its *A*-time from future to present to past. We *B*-theorists deny this; but we do not deny that my seeing what Jim is doing before, during and after the race can make me believe successively, and truly, that his race is future, present and past. And similarly for all other perceptible examples of time flowing. We can experience all of them just as easily – and as truly – without the flow of time as with it. So our undeniably real experience of time flowing gives us no reason to think that it flows in reality.

7 *McTaggart's proof*

1 Change and the flow of time

In the last two chapters I set out to discredit three discreditable inferences often drawn from the *B*-theory of time. Now I set out to discredit the rival *A*-theory by discrediting its account of change. Change is clearly of time's essence, and many have thought it the downfall of all *B*-theories – that only an *A*-theory can account for it. In fact the opposite is true. What disproves all *A*-theories is a contradiction inherent in their concept of change.

Change, obviously if vaguely, is something having a property at one time and not at another. More precisely, it is a thing having incompatible properties, like different temperatures or *B*-places, at different *B*-times. Cooling is a change of temperature, being first hot and then cold; movement a change of place, being first at one place and then at another. Likewise for changes of size, shape, colour and other properties. In all cases of change something has one of a number of mutually incompatible properties at one *B*-time and another one later.

Although this *B*-theory of change will prove in the end to be as right as it is obvious, it does face two serious charges. The first is that it cannot say why we should distinguish change over time from change across space. Properties can after all vary from place to place as well as from time to time. Think of a poker, with one end in the fire, that is simultaneously hot at that end and cold at the other end. Why is this not as much a case of change as the whole poker being hot at 2.15 and cold at 3.15?

We could say of course that this is just what our concept of change is: variation over time. But why should our concept exclude spatial variation? And how, if it does, can we distinguish time from the dimensions of space, as we saw in chapter 5 that we must? To distinguish time as the dimension of change will be circular if we limit change to temporal variation merely by definition. Yet how else are we to distinguish it?

Consider again a clock's second hand passing successively the figures '1' and '2'. The latter event is both later than the former and to the right of it. We see this as change (in this case movement), which is how we distinguish the temporal and spatial relations of the two events. Specifically, it is how we tell a thin hand moving over the clock face from a fat one spread statically across it in two spatial dimensions. In short, we see the temporal relation in this case by seeing change.

Similarly for our perceptions of all other changes, and indeed of time order generally. To see that one event is later than another is mostly if not always to see something change. How else then can time be seen or understood, if not as the dimension of change? But change cannot then be defined independently as variation over time. And the charge facing our *B*-theory of time is that, having no other way of defining change, it reduces the temporal nature of change to a trivial tautology.

This charge is reinforced by the other one, namely that our *B*-theory reduces change to changeless facts. If a poker is hot at 2.15 and cold at 3.15, then those always were and always will be its temperatures at those times. These *B*-facts no more change over time than spatial *B*-facts change across space. But what stops a poker's being hot at one end and cold at the other being a case of change is precisely that its hot and cold ends coexist in a single world, albeit in different *B*-places. But then, as we saw in chapter 2, on a *B*-theory the hot poker and the cold also coexist in a single world, albeit at different *B*-times. So if, as everyone agrees, coexistence rules out change in the spatial case, how can it be compatible with change in time?

A-theorists have an easy answer to this question. Change for them derives from the flow of time, whose spatial analogue does not exist in reality. *B*-places are all there is to space; but *B*-times are not all there is to time: there is also an ever-changing present. What makes my clock hand's movement change is that its passing '1' and '2' become successively present, and similarly for all other changes.

Change for *A*-theorists is the successive presence of different events, which in turn determines their time order: one event is earlier than another if and only if it is present first. If by contrast there is in reality no such thing as being spatially present, then there is no spatial analogue of this. The spatial analogues of the earlier–later relation must then be *sui generis*, and that is the difference between space and time. In time but not in space, the *B*-series follows from the *A*-series, and this is what makes temporal but not spatial variation change. Change may still be defined as variation over time, but by defining time first as the dimension that flows, *A*-theorists stop this definition of change begging the question against its spatial counterparts.

This *A*-theory of change may be further buttressed by doctrines about what else turns on temporal presence. There is the view that existence turns on it, i.e. that coming to be present is coming to exist. This makes time even more different from space by making it the dimension in which events come into (and perhaps go out of) existence. Still, whatever else turns on it, the question here is whether the ever-changing present really does explain the existence and temporal nature of change; and, appearances to the contrary, the fact is that it does not.

To start with, we might accuse *A*-theorists too of begging the question against spatial change by denying the existence of *A*-places. These after all vary across space just as *A*-times vary over time. If change is different events being temporally present at different times, why should it not also be different things being spatially present at different places?

To this accusation some *A*-theorists reply that we have a direct intuition of temporal but not of spatial presence, because our senses show events to us as temporally but not as spatially present. This enables us to see the *B*-places of events independently of their *A*-places, whereas we do *not* see their *B*-times independently of their *A*-times. But this, as we saw in chapter 1.5, is not true: we do see the *B*-times of events independently of their *A*-times. And while what I called in chapter 6.4 'our default habit of believing events to happen ... as we see them' has indeed no spatial analogue, what explains this, as we saw there, is not the flow of time but the speed of light.

However, although we might well convict the *A*-theory of change of distinguishing time from space no better than the *B*-theory, I shall press that point no further. It is superfluous to prefer debatable and relatively trifling charges when we can prove our opponents guilty of a capital offence, namely self-contradiction; a charge of which *A*-theories of both time and space are guilty. But as no one will defend the *A*-theory of space, I need only prefer the charge of contradiction in the temporal case.

2 The contradiction in the flow of time

The proof of contradiction in the *A*-theory of change is not new. It was given by McTaggart in his (1908) paper and has been hotly debated ever since. To me it seems beyond all reasonable doubt, but as it is still disputed, I fear I must present it yet again.

Two factors make me hope for more success than McTaggart had. One is that he attacked time itself. He thought that time needs change, and that change needs the flow of time, whose impossibility he took to show that time does not exist. The incredibility of this conclusion unfortunately made his whole argument suspect. Time's flow has been wrongly acquitted to save the innocent time.

But we need not acquit the guilty in this case in order to save the innocent. What is wrong with McTaggart is not his attack on time's flow but his view that change requires it. I shall show this in chapter 8 by giving a *B*-theory which distinguishes change from spatial variation without invoking the flow of time. Given such a theory, we can deny the reality of *A*-times without denying reality to either change or time. That should make McTaggart's proof much more acceptable.

The other factor is the *B*-theory of *A*-truth and *A*-belief outlined in chapters 3 to 6. Although not much of this is new, none of it was there in McTaggart's time, and it too should make his proof more persuasive. On the one hand it should make the proof's validity more obvious and, on the other, its conclusions more palatable. In particular, as we saw in chapter 6.4, the flow of time is not being banished entirely, merely put back where it belongs – in our minds.

McTaggart's proof is simple. Many *A*-times are incompatible with each other. An event which is yesterday, for example, cannot also be tomorrow, because past, present and future, as defined in chapter 1.2, are mutually incompatible *A*-times. Yet because each event is always changing its *A*-times, it has to have them all. But nothing can really have incompatible properties, so nothing in reality has these *A*-times. The *A*-series is a myth.

The defence has an immediate and obvious riposte to this attack, whose rebuttal is unfortunately far less obvious, which is why McTaggart's proof has rarely carried the conviction it deserves. The riposte is that nothing has incompatible *A*-times at the same time. Nothing is present when it is past, or future when it is present. Events have these *A*-times only in succession, being at first future, then present, and then past, but never all at once. And nothing prevents anything having incompatible properties at different times. On the contrary, that is what change is: the successive possession of incompatible properties. All McTaggart has shown is that changes of *A*-time fit the definition, as they should.

To rebut this riposte, McTaggart asks when, in *A*-terms, events have their various *A*-times; and here it will help to use some symbols. Let *P*, *N* and *F* be respectively the *A*-times past, present (now) and future, and let *e* be any event. Then *e*'s being past, present and future I write respectively as '*Pe*', '*Ne*' and '*Fe*'. Complexes of these simple *A*-times are represented by repeated ascriptions of *P*, *N* and *F*: thus '*PFe*' means that *e was* future, '*FPNe*' means that *e will have been* present, and so on. '~', '&' and '⊨' mean respectively 'not', 'and' and 'entails'.

Then McTaggart's basic argument is that while the three times *P*, *N* and *F* are mutually incompatible, so that

(5) $Pe \models {\sim}Ne$; $Ne \models {\sim}Fe$; $Fe \models {\sim}Pe$; etc.,

the flow of time requires every event to have all three of them, i.e.

(6) $Pe \;\&\; Ne \;\&\; Fe$.

But (5) and (6) cannot both be true; since if (6) is true, two of the entailments in (5) fail, making (5) false. But our *A*-concept of time commits us to both (5) and (6); so it entails a contradiction and cannot apply to reality. In reality therefore time cannot flow, because there can be no *A*-facts.

To this the riposte is that *e* has no more than one of these incompatible *A*-times at once, so there is no contradiction after all. Suppose for example that *e* is present: *Ne*. Then *e* is neither past nor future, so that both '*Pe*' and '*Fe*' are false, as (5) requires. What is true is that *e will be* past and *was* future, i.e. not (6) but

(7) $FPe \mathbin{\&} Ne \mathbin{\&} PFe$,

which is quite compatible with (5).

So it is. But, as McTaggart says, there are more complex *A*-times than those in (7), and not all combinations of them are compatible. Specifically, there are also *PP* and *PN*, *FF* and *FN*, and *NP*, *NN* and *NF*. And just as every event has all simple *A*-times if it has any, so it also has all these complex *A*-times. For example, whatever has any simple *A*-time obviously has it *now*, so that

$$Pe \vDash NPe;\ Ne \vDash NNe;\ Fe \vDash NFe.$$

Obviously too, whatever is past *was* present and *was* future, and whatever is future *will be* present and *will be* past, so that

$$Pe \vDash PNe;\ Pe \vDash PFe;\ Fe \vDash FNe;\ Fe \vDash FPe.$$

Moreover, whatever is sufficiently past also *was* past (e.g. what happened two days ago was already past yesterday), and events that are sufficiently future now *will be* future in the future, which gives us *PP* and *FF*.

So instead of three simple *A*-times, we now have nine complex ones: *PP*, *PN*, *PF*; *NP*, *NN*, *NF*; *FP*, *FN*, *FF*. But McTaggart's argument applies equally to them. Since the *A*-times of events are always changing, every event that has any of these nine complex *A*-times must have all of them; but not all of them are compatible. For example, *FF* and *PP* are incompatible, since what will be future cannot also have been past. And *NP*, *NN* and *NF* are obviously incompatible, being equivalent to the simple *P*, *N* and *F*.

The riposte will again be made, that *e* does not have these incompatible *A*-times all at once. But again, saying in *A*-terms just when they do have them simply generates even more complex *A*-times, including mutually incompatible ones like *PPP*, *NNN* and *FFF*, all of which every event has to have. In short, we have an endless regress, a regress that is vicious because at no stage in it can all the *A*-facts it entails be consistently stated.

3 In defence of McTaggart

This, basically, is how McTaggart put his case. His critics react by denying the viciousness of his regress. At every stage, they say, we can remove the apparent contradiction by distinguishing the times at which events have incompatible *A*-times. They ignore the fact that the way they distinguish these times, by iterating their ascriptions of *A*-times, only generates more contradictions. However, the debate is too well worn by now to be settled by simply repeating McTaggart's proof, sound though it is. To change the metaphor, too many people have managed to inoculate themselves against it. So if it is to wipe out belief in *A*-facts, as it should, we need a more virulent strain of it, a strain which I think is best nurtured on the *B*-facts that make *A*-propositions true or false.

Before developing the new strain, however, I should neutralise some antidotes peddled by *A*-theorists to McTaggart's original proof. And first I should note that although I have only discussed the unqualified past, present and future, the proof applies also to more precise *A*-times. *Yesterday* and *three days ago*, for example, are incompatible *A*-times of events that last less than a day, both of which all such events must nevertheless have. But we need not complicate the proof by bringing all *A*-times into it explicitly. All parties will agree that if it works for *P*, *N* and *F*, it will work for all *A*-times; and if not, for none.

Second, I have followed McTaggart in ascribing *A*-times to events. As I noted in chapter 3.5, tense logicians prefer to treat '*P*', '*N*' and '*F*' as so-called *operators* (analogous to 'It is possible that ...') prefixed to core now-sentences. This in effect treats *P*, *N* and *F* as *A*-times of *A*-facts rather than of events. Thus where McTaggart and I start with a storm, tense logicians start with a storm's happening now. Where we say the storm is two days past, they say that its happening now is two days past. In my symbolism, this amounts to replacing '*e*' throughout by '*Ne*'. But it makes no odds to the proof, as readers may verify for themselves. Facts are no better than events at being at once both and not both past and present, present and future, etc.

Nor does it help to distinguish a so-called *object language*, the language we use to say that events or facts are past, present or future, from its *meta-language*, the language we use to say which object language sentences are true. Or rather, it helps only if we use *B*-sentences in the meta-language to say when object language *A*-sentences are true. But this is to give these *A*-sentences *B*-truth-conditions, which are no use to *A*-theorists, who must therefore use *A*-sentences in the meta-language too.

But this only generates a variant of McTaggart's proof, with truth and falsity as the incompatible properties. For all the true *A*-sentences that concern us are also (sometimes) false. This is the new basic contradiction, and the riposte to it is the same: no object language *A*-sentence is both true and false at the same time. And by using sentences in the meta-language to say when our object language *A*-sentences are true and when they are false, we can show that they imply no contradiction.

But if these meta-language sentences are *A*-sentences, they too will be both true and false: the contradiction simply recurs in the meta-language. And removing it from there by using *A*-sentences in a meta-meta-language to say when the meta-language ones are true just sets up the next stage of McTaggart's vicious regress. McTaggart's proof can no more be evaded by iterating meta-languages than it can by iterating *A*-operators (or the ascriptions of *A*-times to events or *A*-facts) in the object language.

The plain fact is that nothing can have mutually incompatible properties, whether they be *A*-times or truth values: not events, facts, propositions, sentences or anything else. So I will continue to put McTaggart's proof in terms of events, in the broad sense of chapter 1.2. To reformulate it in other idioms only fosters the illusion that some such reformulation can show it to be fallacious.

Third, I must meet the charge that my symbolic version of McTaggart's proof begs the question against *A*-theorists. The point is that in using '*Pe*' to say that *e* is past, I have left out the verb 'is'. By so doing I have tacitly treated the 'is' in '*e* is past' as a tenseless copula, and this is what makes *e*'s being past, present and future seem contradictory. But the verb 'is' in '*e* is past' is present tense, i.e. it really means that *e* is *now* past, which removes the contradiction. For if *e* is now past, it is not also now present or now future. Of course, it *was* present and *was* future, but that is perfectly compatible with *e* being now past. In short, the apparent contradiction is an artefact of my system, generated by suppressing the present tense of the verb we use to ascribe to events the *A*-times *P*, *N* and *F*.

This charge misses the point completely. The *A*-series is meant to be a feature of the world, not of verbs. Yet the habit of calling *A*-times 'tenses' both reflects and abets a persistent confounding of the two that still vitiates much philosophy of time, and is manifest in the present charge. This is why I have not only given up the habit but will now, in order to meet the charge and try to dispel the confusion, say something about how we do, but need not, use verbal tenses to ascribe *A*-times.

English lets us use verbal tenses on their own to ascribe basic *A*-times, as in 'Jim runs', which says that his running is present or future, and 'Jim ran', which says that it is past. English also has some adverbs and phrases, like 'now', 'in the future' and 'in the past', which do the same thing, and others, like 'today', 'next week' and 'yesterday', which pick out more precise *A*-times. And when we use any of these adverbial expressions, we modify the verb to match, as in 'Jim *ran* in the past', 'Jim *runs* today', 'Jim *runs* (or *will run*) next week', and so on.

Using an adverbial expression to give an *A*-time, however, makes the use of a matching verbal tense redundant. Grammar may require it, but it adds no temporal information. If it did, it would give past and future tense sentences meanings they do not have: it would make 'Jim *ran* yesterday' mean that yesterday he ran at an even earlier time, 'Jim *will run* next week' mean that next week he will run at an even later time, and so on.

Similarly, unless '*e* was past' and '*e* will be future' are to mean that *e* was past *in the past* (*PP*) and will be future *in the future* (*FF*), the modifications of 'is' in these sentences must also be redundant. To say that *e* is past or future *now* we should really say '*e is* past' or '*e is* future', just as we say '*e is* present'. But then the 'is' in all these sentences *is* a mere tenseless copula, which adds no temporal information and is present only to give the sentences a verb, however vacuous. Nothing therefore is left out when we abbreviate '*e* is past', '*e* is present' and '*e* is future' to '*Pe*', '*Ne*' and '*Fe*' respectively. But if nothing is left out, the abbreviation can create no contradiction which was not already there.

Anyone who still says that the 'is' in '*e* is past' is present tense, i.e. that it makes '*e* is past' mean '*e* is *now* past', must then say what tense 'is' has in '*e* is now past'. It is clearly either tenseless or present tense, and if tenseless, McTaggart's proof is restored at once, since '*e* is now past' is not always true. It is true when, and only when, '*e* is past' is true (which is why the two sentences are synonymous). But then, as readers may easily verify, we can apply McTaggart's proof to it by replacing '*P*', '*N*' and '*F*' throughout by '*NP*', '*NN*' and '*NF*'.

But if the 'is' in '*e* is now past' is present tense, as in '*e* is past', the same vicious regress appears in the sentence itself. For '*e* is past', meaning '*e* is now past', must now also mean '*e* is now now past', in which the 'is' must again be either tenseless or present tense. If it is tenseless, we again get McTaggart's proof, starting this time with '*NNP*', '*NNN*' and '*NNF*'; and if it is present tense, the regress continues with '*e* is now now now past', 'e is now now now now past', and so on for ever.

And to no sentence in this endless sequence can we give consistent *A*-truth-conditions. It is no use saying at any stage that the latest sentence is true *now*, since whether that is so depends on when *now* is. Saying this merely generates the next sentence in the sequence, about which the same question arises. To give a final answer at any stage just produces a contradiction, since if the sentence is true (at some present time) it is also false (at some other). The only way to avoid contradiction is never to stop at all, thus admitting in effect that the original sentence, '*e* is past', has *no A*-truth-conditions. But this is to say that no *A*-fact, and so in particular not the fact that *e* is past, makes '*e* is past' true. In short, *A*-facts are either self-contradictory or incapable of making *A*-sentences true or false. Yet that is what they are defined to do. So either way they do not exist.

4 McTaggart and truth-conditions

So much for McTaggart's own proof. But in case it still does not convince when put in his way, I will now put it explicitly in terms of truthmakers. First, recall that *A*-facts are meant to provide single truthmakers for *A*-propositions. Just as 'Snow is white' is made true at all places and times by the single fact that snow is white, so '*e* is past' is meant to be made true by the single fact that *e* is past. However much its *B*-truth-condition varies from time to time, its *A*-truth-condition is always that *e* is past.

All parties also agree however that, for any event *e*, '*e* is past' is true at all *B*-times later than *e* and false at all other times. So if the *A*-fact that *e* is past is to be the truthmaker for '*e* is past', that is when this *A*-fact must exist. And when it does so, it must make true not only this proposition but also all its tokens, thus requiring all tokens of '*e* is past' to have the same truth value at any one time, namely to be true if the time is after *e* and otherwise false. For if at any time different tokens of '*e* is past' differed in truth value, they would need different truthmakers, and '*e* is past' and its tokens would not be made true by a single fact.

Now consider two tokens, *a* and *b*, of '*e* is past', one earlier than *e* and one later. Suppose for example that *e* is Jim's race on 2 June, which unknown to me has been postponed from 2.30 to 4.30; that *a* is my saying '*e* is past' prematurely at 3.30; and that *b* is my saying it again at 5.30. Then if *a* and *b* are both made true by the *A*-fact that *e* is past, they must both be true when this *is* a fact and false when it is not. So at 4 p.m., when *e* is still future, *a* and *b* must both be false; and at 5 p.m., when it is past, they must both be true. These truth values are marked '(I)' in Figure 5 opposite.

Yet they are obviously wrong. To say *before* Jim's race that it is past is to produce a token of '*e* is past' that is and always will be false. Similarly, to say *after* his race that it is past is to produce a token that is and always was true. Hence the truth values marked '(II)' in Figure 5.

These must be the right truth values. Once we distinguish propositions from their tokens, it is obvious that tokens of an *A*-proposition, unlike the proposition itself, do *not* change their truth values over time. (We may ignore special cases, like the 'Back in two hours' sign of chapter 3.1.) No one thinks, for example, that my death will posthumously verify every

	Past	Present		Future
	2.30	3.30	4.30	5.30
***A*-series at 4 p.m.**				
e is not past			***e***	
Tokens of '*e* is past'		***a***		***b***
Truth values (I)		False		False
Truth values (II)		False		True
	3.30	4.30	5.30	6.30
***A*-series at 5 p.m.**				
e is past		***e***		
Tokens of '*e* is past'	***a***		***b***	
Truth values (I)	True		True	
Truth values (II)	False		True	

Figure 5

premature announcement of it! Nor, to draw a spatial analogy, does anyone in London take the token 'London 60' on a signpost in Cambridge to be false just because it *would* be false in London. And if, in the personal case, I denied your statement 'I am in pain' because *I* was not in pain, that could only show that I did not know what 'I' means.

Similarly, those who would say that *e*'s occurrence makes previously false tokens of '*e* is past' true are losing their grip on what 'past', 'present' and 'future' mean. Specifically, they are confounding the obviously true thesis (A), stated in chapter 3.3, that

> the truth value of any token *u* of any proposition 'P' [is] the truth value 'P' has for whomever produces *u* when and where they do so,

with the thesis (B) that *u*'s truth value at any time is just the truth value which 'P' has at that time. But (B) must be false, simply because the *A*-propositions that concern us are true at some times and not at others. So any tokens of such a proposition that had to share its truth value at all times would have to be both true and false. This is McTaggart's contradiction, expressed in a way that allows no regress and hence no riposte.

Note that *A*-theorists cannot save (B) by making the truth values of tokens of *A*-propositions like '*e* is past' vary from time to time. For not only, as we have just seen, do they *not* so vary, making them do so reduces (A) to a mere special case of (B), which is absurd. It puts the falsehood of my statement 'Jim's race is past' at 4 p.m. on a par with its truth value at any other time, as if this token's own temporal location was not what made it false. No one who grasps the distinction between a proposition and its tokens can believe that.

I conclude therefore that we must reject (B) and admit that tokens of '*e* is past' like *a* and *b* can and do have different truth values at a given time. But then they cannot all be made true at that time by a single fact, neither the fact that *e* is past nor any other. Let us see if *A*-theorists can accept this.

Suppose it is now 6 p.m. on the day of Jim's 4.30 race (*e*), so that *e* is now past. This fact is not enough to make all tokens of '*e* is past' true now: my 5.30 token *b* is true now; but my 3.30 token *a* is not. Can we say what *A*-facts, if not the fact that *e* is past, make *a* false and *b* true? On the face of it we can. What makes *a* false is that it is *more past* than *e*, and what makes *b* true is that it is *less past* than *e*. Similarly, with suitable variations, for all other times and all other tokens of '*e* is past'. In general, any token *u* of '*e* is past' is true at any *A*- or *B*-time *t* if and only if *u* is less past or more future than *e*; and similarly for all other *A*-propositions, as readers may again verify for themselves.

These truthmakers are fine – except that they are *B*-facts, not *A*-facts. We saw in chapter 1.3 that the same earlier–later relation orders events and *B*-times in both *A*- and *B*-series. What makes events past at any *A*- or *B*-time *t* is that they are earlier than *t*, and what makes them future at *t* is that they are later than *t*. So what makes '*a* is more past or less future than *e*' true at any time *t* is the *B*-fact that *a* is earlier than *e*; just as what makes '*b* is less past or more future than *e*' true at *t* is that *b* is later than *e*.

In both cases, therefore, the *A*- or *B*-time *t* cancels out, which is why neither '*a* is more past or less future than *e*' nor '*b* is less past or more future than *e*' can be true at one time and false at another. This in turn is why time flows at the same rate for all events, i.e. never changes their relative positions in the *A*-series, because they all get less future and more past at the same tautological rate of sixty minutes per hour.

And this is what reduces the apparent *A*-truthmaker for any token of '*e* is past' to the *B*-truthmaker that the token be later than *e*. The token *b* is true (at all times) because it is later than *e*, and *a* is false (at all times) because it is not. That, as shown opposite in Figure 6, is all there is to it. The *A*-times of *e*, *a* and *b* are irrelevant.

In short, the supposed *A*-fact that *e* is past is no part of what makes any token of '*e* is past' true. Yet this fact's only function – the only reason to postulate it – is to make this *A*-proposition and its tokens true. But that job is already done by *B*-facts like those stated in chapter 6.1 and those depicted in Figure 6. Provided a token *u* of '*e* is past' is later than *e*, it is true. Nothing else about *e* and *u* matters a jot; and in particular no *A*-fact about them matters. It is immaterial where *e* and *u* are in the *A*-series; and

***B*-series**	Earlier	3.30	4.30	5.30	Later
			e		
Tokens of '*e* is past'		*a*		*b*	
Truth values		False		True	

Figure 6

if that is not material, then obviously no other *A*-fact can be. Similarly for all other *A*-propositions and their tokens. Their *B*-truthmakers leave *A*-facts no scope for making them true or false. Yet that, as I said at the end of §3, is what they are defined to do. So in reality there are no such facts.

5 A growing *B*-world?

McTaggart's proof disposes of more than *A*-facts. It disposes also of the idea, mentioned in chapter 2.1, that even *B*-facts need not exist at all times. Specifically, the idea is that *B*-facts about any event *e* come into existence only when *e* does. So, for example, until Jim races on 2 June, it is a fact neither that he races then nor that he does not. It follows that neither 'Jim races on 2 June' nor 'Jim does not race on 2 June' is true on 1 June, since neither of the facts that would make these *B*-propositions true exists then.

This is an initially attractive *B*-theory surrogate for the *A*-theory that only what is present or past exists, and is developed as such in Tooley (1997). It lets present events and *B*-facts (and hence the present *B*-time) be defined, without invoking any *A*-facts, as the latest events and *B*-facts, i.e. as those such that no later events or facts exist. The present is thus defined as the boundary between what exists and what does not, a boundary that moves continuously as more events and *B*-facts come into existence.

This theory obviously avoids many of the objections to *A*-facts; but not all. First, by linking presence, and hence simultaneity, to existence, it falls foul of special relativity and modern cosmology, for the reasons outlined in chapter 5.6. What exists elsewhere in the universe as you read this sentence cannot depend on assumptions (about our absolute velocity) all of which, if these theories are right, lack truthmakers. Any moving boundary between what exists and what does not must, at any *B*-time, extend as a matter of fact across the whole of space. Anyone accepting this theory must therefore, as Tooley admits, do so in the teeth of modern physics.

The theory also falls foul of McTaggart. For what after all does it mean to say that events (and *B*-facts and *B*-times) exist at some *B*-times and not at others? It cannot just mean that events have (i.e. are located at) specific *B*-times, e.g. that Jim's race has a short *B*-time *t* starting at 4.30. To infer that only at *t* does this event or *B*-fact *exist*, meaning that only at *t* is 'Jim races at *t*' *true*, is in effect to be a presentist: to say that events exist only while they are present. And this theory says no such thing, since it requires 'Jim races at *t*' to be true, and hence Jim's racing at *t* to exist, at *B*-times later than *t*.

What then can *B*-theorists mean by '*e* exists at *t*', if not that *t* is (or is in) *e*'s *B*-time? They cannot mean that, at *t*, *e* exists *now*, or *in the past*, since these are *A*-facts. Nor can existing be a property that *e* can have at some times and lack at others, like Jim's property of racing. For to have or lack this property at any time Jim must at least be located at that time. But then *e*'s existing at times *after* its *B*-time cannot be a property it has at those times, since it is not *at* those times to have that (or any other) property. Similarly, *e*'s *not* existing at times *before* its *B*-time cannot be its lacking at those times the property of existence, since it is not at those times to lack it.

Nor can existing be a property, like being famous, that entities can have or lack before or after their *B*-times. For these are not really properties of – in the sense of constituents of truthmaking facts about – the entities we ascribe them to. What makes '*e* is famous at *t*' true for any entity *e* and *B*-time *t* is that many people at *t* think about *e*, and these are facts about those people, not about *e*. This is what enables *e* to be famous at *t* without existing at any time (like Sherlock Holmes), let alone at *t*. But existence is not like this: no facts about entities other than *e* and *t* will make '*e* exists at *t*' true if facts about *e* and *t* do not.

Yet how can facts about *t* affect the truth value of '*e* exists at *t*' if, as we have agreed, this does not mean that *e* is located at *t*? If it did mean that, it would be like '*e* exists at *s*', where *s* is *e*'s *B*-place; and if it does not, then *t* is no more relevant to its truth than *s* is. But if the existential proposition is just '*e* exists', a *B*-proposition whose only truthmaker is *e* itself, what can make this true at one time and not at another? It cannot be the fact that *e* exists at one time and not at another if time is no part of the proposition to be made true: the only relevant fact is that *e* exists. So if '*e* exists' is ever true it is always true. And on this theory '*e* exists' *is* true at all times at and after *e*'s *B*-time *t*. But then at no earlier time can it either be false or lack a truth value, or it would be both true and not true, which is impossible.

That this is a version of McTaggart's contradiction we can see by considering the obvious riposte to it, namely that '*e* exists' is not both true and not true at the same time. It is true at and after *t*, when *e* exists, and not true before *t*, when *e* does not exist, and there is no contradiction in that.

To see the reply to this riposte we must ask, as in §4, what gives tokens of '*e* exists' their truth values. Take again the example of Jim's racing at 4.30 p.m., and consider our growing world at 4 and 5 p.m., as shown in

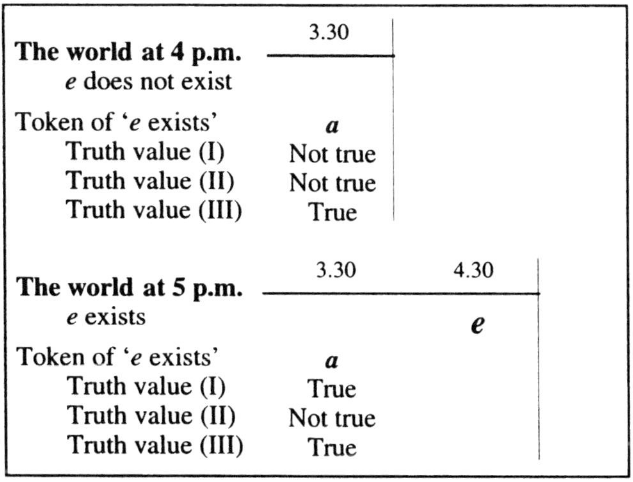

Figure 7

Figure 7. Suppose moreover that at 3.30 I say '*e* exists', i.e. 'Jim races at 4.30', and call this token of that *B*-proposition '*a*'. If what makes '*e* exists' and its tokens true is the fact that *e* exists, then at 4 p.m., when *e* does not exist, *a* is *not* true, and at 5 p.m., when *e* does exist, it *is* true: hence the truth values marked '(I)' in Figure 7.

But these must be wrong, even on Tooley's theory. For to say *before* Jim's race that it exists, when it does not, is to produce a token of '*e* exists' that is not, and never will be, true. Hence the truth values marked '(II)'. To suppose that *a* becomes true when *e* comes to exist is, as noted in §4, to confound a token of the proposition '*e* exists' with the proposition itself.

However, if the arguments of §4 show that *a* cannot *become* true, they do not show that it *is* not true. On the contrary. For what '*e* exists' and all its tokens say, with no temporal qualification, is that *e* exists. But then the fact that *e does* exist at some time or other must suffice to make the *B*-proposition which says so true at all times. And this, by thesis (A) of §4 (that the truth value of any token *u* of any proposition 'P' is the truth value 'P' has for whomever produces *u* when and where they do so), makes *a* and all other tokens of '*e* exists' true, whenever they occur.

Hence the truth values marked '(III)' in Figure 7: '*e* exists' and all its tokens are true at all times. But this means that it is a fact at all times that *e* exists, and similarly for all other events, *B*-facts and *B*-times: the number of them never changes. The universe may be expanding in the sense of being larger at later times than it is at earlier ones; but it is not growing by the addition of events or *B*-facts.

8 *Change*

1 The *B*-theory of change

For time to flow is for events, *B*-facts and *B*-times to have *A*-times that change from future to present to past. But, as we have just seen, this kind of change entails a contradiction and so cannot really occur. This means that the *A*-theory of change outlined in chapter 7.1 must be false. We must therefore either meet the objections given there to the rival *B*-theory or conclude with McTaggart that in reality there is no change.

In chapter 7.1 I cited two objections to the *B*-theory that a change is a thing having incompatible properties at different *B*-times. These are that the theory has no way of distinguishing properties varying over time from properties varying across space, and that it reduces changes to changeless facts. The short answer to these objections is that the first is false and the second is not an objection. For why, to take the second one first, must facts change in order to *be* changes? If for example the relevant facts are that a poker is hot at 2.15 and cold at 3.15, why can these facts not constitute a change in the poker, just because they always were and always will be facts?

The first objection is false because *B*-theorists need not invoke change to distinguish time from space. They can use causation to do this, since time is the only dimension in which causes are always separated from – by being earlier than – their effects. Why this is so we shall see in chapter 10; for the time being we may simply assume that it is so, and therefore that time can be defined as the causal dimension of spacetime. The question then is why we distinguish properties varying over this dimension from properties varying over the other dimensions of spacetime, a question I shall answer in §7.

But first I must develop the *B*-theory of change. It is not enough to say that changes are things having incompatible properties at different times. To meet apparent counter-examples to this definition we shall need to set limits both to things and to properties, and of course to set them without any question-begging appeal to change. That is the business of the next two sections.

2 Events and things

In chapter 1.2 I said that for the time being I would call all entities located in time (other than times) 'events'. Now however we need to restrict the term 'event' to draw some necessary distinctions. First we must distinguish truthmaking facts, like the fact that Jim races on 2 June, from so-called *particulars*, like Jim. Facts correspond to sentences, like 'Jim races', which they make true; particulars correspond to names, like 'Jim', and descriptions, like 'my racing friend', which on their own tell us nothing either true or false.

Next we must distinguish two sorts of particulars, only one of which, I shall argue, is capable of change. These are what I shall call *things*, such as nations, firms, people, animals and plants, and inanimate objects ranging in size from quarks to clusters of galaxies. The other, unchangeable, sort of particulars are what in my restricted sense I shall call *events*, such as Jim's and other races, elections, meals, speeches, collisions, and so on.

Whatever our views of the changeability of things and events, we should all agree that these are distinct sorts of particulars. For however we think they differ, there will be little doubt or dispute about which other kinds of particulars go with those that I have just called things and which go with those that I have called events.

Many philosophers, however, who admit the distinction, deny the reality of events like Jim's race, saying that the only particular constituent of the fact that Jim races is Jim himself. I disagree, for reasons I shall give in chapter 9 but need not anticipate here. For as my *B*-theory of change will apply only to things, it will not really matter to it if there are no events. But since I think there are events, I should say why the theory does not apply to them. This means saying how events differ from things, and why the difference makes events unchangeable.

How then do events differ from things? The short answer is that things, unlike events, even when extended in time, lack temporal parts. They may of course have spatial parts, like the atoms that are parts of molecules, the limbs and other parts of our bodies, the sun, planets and other parts of our solar system, and so on. And so may events, such as a family meal, whose spatial parts are the meals eaten by each member of the family. In this respect things and events are alike.

The fact is that all particulars whose properties vary across space have spatial parts. By this I mean that no smaller part of the place occupied at any one time by such a particular ever contains more than a part of it (and many parts of that place – such as the empty spaces between the particles postulated by the kinetic theory of gases – may contain none of it). At no time is a molecule wholly present in the place wholly occupied at that time by one of its atoms, nor is the solar system ever wholly present in the place wholly occupied at that time by the sun, and so on.

By contrast, not all particulars extended in time have temporal parts. Events do: each course of a meal is a temporal part of it. But things do not: atoms, people and planets have only spatial parts. This means that things, unlike events, *are* wholly present at every moment within their *B*-times. Some *B*-theorists admittedly deny this, for reasons given in §5, and credit all temporally extended entities with temporal parts; but no one else does. No one else would say that only parts of Sir Edmund Hillary and Tenzing Norgay climbed only a part of Everest in 1953. The rest of us think those two whole men climbed that one whole mountain, and that all three parties were wholly present throughout every temporal part of that historic event.

Likewise, when Churchill published an account of his early life, that is what he called it: *My Early Life*, not *Early Me*. Similarly with all other natural and social things. No one thinks a committee has temporal parts, just because its meetings do, or that a hailstone has, just because its falling is a temporal as well as a spatial part of a hailstorm. Nor do physicists take only temporal parts of an electron and a positron to vanish when the two collide: the two whole particles are what they take to collide and disappear.

Everyone, on the other hand, credits events with temporal parts. The rapidly successive stages of explosions, for example, are distinguished and described in theories of the subject, just as geologists detect and describe epochs in the evolution of the earth. On an intermediate human scale we have the courses that are parts of meals, the single steps that are parts of races, and so on. Historians similarly are always picking out crucial stages of historical events; although never, be it noted, of nations or peoples. Thus they all credit the French Revolution with temporal parts, but not France herself, or the French people.

So far so good. The temporal-parts test works well for most if not all kinds of temporal particular, as I hope readers will agree. The kinds we would all classify with my examples of things are the very kinds we take to be wholly present at more than one time, just as the kinds we take to have temporal parts are those we would all classify with my examples of events.

Naturally more needs saying, especially about instantaneous particulars, like spacetime points, to which the temporal-parts test does not apply. But spacetime points and regions need distinguishing anyway from other particulars located at them, so I shall call them neither things nor events. Other instantaneous particulars I shall call events rather than things, in order to preserve two useful implications: (i) that no events are things, and (ii) that things are wholly present at more than one time and so can be reidentified as such from time to time.

More also needs saying about the concept of a part. For if parts needed only spacetime boundaries, then we could give things temporal parts by mere definition, like Jim-in-June. But by 'part' I mean more than this. I mean what we all mean by spatial parts, like parts of our bodies: namely, things or events whose existence is logically independent of the wholes they are parts of. Unless 'Jim-in-June' picks out such an entity – which I deny – Jim-in-June is no part of Jim in my sense since, unlike his limbs, it could not exist without him. Each step of Jim's race, by contrast, could exist on its own, and so is as much a part of his race as his limbs are of his body.

And as for parts, so for wholes. They too must be things or events in their own right: their existence must not be entailed merely by that of the things or events which are in fact their parts. This means in particular that I will not identify any thing or event that has parts with the so-called *mereological sum* of the things or events that are its parts; since this entity, if it exists at all (which I doubt), exists if its parts do by mere definition.

3 Changes and properties

So much for the time being for how things differ from events, a difference which, as we shall see, confines changes to temporal variations in the properties of things. But before I can say why it does so, I must first limit the range of changeable properties, just as I have limited the range of changeable particulars.

Our *B*-theory says that a thing changes when its properties change, i.e. when it has incompatible properties at different *B*-times. Yet it is obvious that not every change in the apparent properties of a thing is a change in that thing. Take the property of being an only child. I cease to have this property when my parents have another child, but that is not a change in me. Or take again the property, cited in chapter 7.5, of being famous. We become or cease to be famous when enough other people start or stop thinking about us; but those are changes in them, not in us. Similarly with other so-called *relational properties*, which things can gain or lose without changing, simply because other things change. Jim, for example, need not change in height to cease to be taller than his growing son Jeff.

What stops all these changes in properties being changes in the things that have those properties is that the first effects of the changes lie elsewhere. The birth of another child to my parents is not a change in me, because its first effects are neither on nor near me. The first effects of changes in our fame are on and near those whose thinking of us makes us famous, so that is where those changes are. The first effects of Jeff's growing to be as tall as Jim are on and near Jeff, not Jim, which is why this change in Jeff is not also a change in Jim. And so on. In short, real changes of properties need effects, and for them to be changes in the things to which we ascribe those properties, that is where their first effects must be.

This causal test of change also yields a causal test for properties that are changeable (and hence contingent, unlike properties of numbers like *being prime*, a restriction I shall take for granted from now on). This is that real changeable properties are those whose changes have their first effects on or near the things we ascribe them to. The idea is that if, for example, changes in my fame are not changes in me, then my being famous is not a property of mine. Yet as it is ascribed to me, it is not a property of anyone or anything else either; so it is not a property at all.

This is why I said in chapter 7.5 that being famous is not a property. What makes '*x* is famous' true for any person *x* is not that *x* has this property, but that many other people have a different one, namely the property of thinking of *x*. It is also why being an only child, being taller than Jeff, and relational properties generally, are not real properties, since properties of *x* do not in general suffice to make '*x* is an only child', '*x* is taller than Jeff', etc., true.

(This is not, I should say, to deny the reality of all contingent *relations* between particulars, like the earlier–later or shorter–taller relations, for which a causal contiguity test will obviously not work. These however need not concern us here; for a general test that covers all contingent properties and relations see my (1991).)

This causal test for properties is related to another one, namely that a thing's properties should be detectable just by inspecting that thing. (This may be disputed for properties like *thinking of Jim*, since arguably nothing detectable in me makes *Jim* the person I am thinking of (Putnam 1975). But then we may well infer, by this very test, that my thinking of Jim is not *just* a property of mine.) For clearly *changes* in a thing's properties will have contiguous effects, including those we use to detect them, if and only if its *having* those properties has contiguous effects. This is why you cannot tell whether I am famous, or an only child, or taller than Jeff, just by looking at me. Your problem is not that these properties of mine are hard to detect, but that you are looking in the wrong place, and hence for properties that do not exist. It takes other properties of other people to make me famous, or an only child, or taller than Jeff.

Other bogus properties our causal test excludes are those made infamous in philosophy by Goodman (1965 chapter 3): *grue*, *bleen* and all their ill-bred mutations. Roughly, to be grue is, up to a certain time *t*, to be green, and thereafter it is to be blue; while 'bleen' is defined the other way round. These properties are bogus because a thing's changing from grue to bleen (i.e. staying green) at *t* is no real change, since it has none of the effects of a change of colour. Whereas a thing's staying grue at t does have the effects of a change of colour, namely those of changing from green to blue, and so it really is a change.

Another temporally defined property which, on a B-theory of time, our test disposes of is *age*. My age is given by the A-time of my birth, and as that gets more past, so my age increases: the flow of time ages us all at the rate of twelve months a year. Yet if in reality time does not flow, ageing so defined cannot be a real change in me or anything else, and cannot therefore have effects. Yet ageing *does* have effects, as we all know. What then, on a B-theory, can ageing be?

The answer is simple enough. To say that people have aged is to say, for example, that sixty years after their births they are in states of physiological decay which most healthy, happy and uninjured people take much longer to reach. The changes which take us from our prime into such states as these are quite real. They have real causes, and real and often unpleasant effects. We may, as with the advancing years themselves, be unable to stop or reverse them; but at least on a B-theory this is a serious and contingent fact of physiology, and not a trivially necessary fact about time.

4 Change, difference and identity

A change, then, is a thing having incompatible real properties at different times. But events, as well as things, can have incompatible properties at different times. Why is that not change? Well, suppose some thing or event a has a pair, F and F', of such properties (e.g. two different temperatures) at two different times t and t'. That is,

(8) a is F at t, and
(8′) a is F' at t'.

If a is an event, it will have different temporal parts spanning t and t': call them p_a and p'_a. Then the apparent change in a consists in the facts that

(9) p_a is F, and
(9′) p'_a is F'.

But now F and F' are properties of different entities, p_a and p'_a, and that stops this being a change, since change needs identity as well as difference. That is, it needs a single particular for the difference to be a change *in*; and here there is no such particular.

To see this, compare p_a and p'_a with Jim and his grandson Jake, who is conceived after Jim dies and has a different blood group. Because Jim and Jake are different people, this difference between them is not a change, even though Jim is a causal ancestor of Jake, they do not overlap in time, and both are parts of the same family. For it is not a change in Jim or Jake, neither of whom ever changes his blood group; nor is it a change in their family, which, as a whole, has no one blood group. So, since it is certainly not a change in anything else, it is not a change at all.

Similarly with p_a and p'_a, neither of which changes, since p_a is only ever F, and p'_a is only ever F'. Nor is the difference between them a change in a, the whole of which p_a and p'_a are parts, since a as a whole is never either F or F'; and nothing can change from having one property to having another if it never has either. And if this difference is not a change in p_a, p'_a or a, it is not a change in anything else either; so it is not a change at all.

In short, differences between temporal parts fail to be changes for the same reason that differences between spatial parts do. Take the poker that is hot at one end and cold at the other. This is not a change in either end, since in neither end is there any difference: one end is all hot and the other is all cold. Nor is it a change in the poker which, as a whole, is neither hot nor cold; and nothing can change from being hot to cold if it is neither. And if this difference is not a change in either the poker or in either of its ends, it is not a change in anything else; so it is not a change at all.

This shows that it need not be by fiat that spatial variation never counts as change. It can be ruled out by an identity condition which, as we have just seen, also stops many temporal variations being changes. The difference between time and space is that, while the condition is *never* met across space, it can be, and often is, met over time; precisely because not all particulars extended in time have temporal parts. Let us see how this helps.

5 Properties as relations to times

If a is a thing, it has no temporal parts to take over its properties F and F'. They are properties of a itself at different times; and this makes them look like relations between a and times. That is, in a common symbolism for relations, it looks as if, when a is a thing, (8) and (8′) should be read, not as (9) and (9′), but as

(10) $F(a,t)$, and
(10′) $F'(a,t')$.

This reading clearly meets our identity condition. It makes F and F' properties of one particular, a, in which the difference between (8) and (8′) can then be a change. Or rather, it makes F and F' *relations* that a has; and there lies the rub. For, as I implied in §3 in distinguishing the changeable properties of things from relations like earlier–later and shorter–taller, these properties seem not to be relations at all. Temperatures, colours, shapes and the like seem to be simple non-relational properties of things.

But if they are, then (10) and (10′) are wrong. The *B*-times *t* and *t′* in (8) and (8′) are not entities that *a* is *related* to by *F* and *F′*, but the temporal *locations* of non-relational facts, *Fa* and *F′a*, which constitute this change. As such, they should be represented by temporal *operators*, as in

(11) at *t*, *Fa*, and
(11′) at *t′*, *F′a*.

To *B*-theorists, however, this poses a problem, because operators are supposed to be prefixed to sentences that express definite propositions. But '*Fa*', read as a *B*-sentence, does not do this. For because *F* is a changeable property, *a* may be *F* at one *B*-time and not at another, as (8) and (8′) say it is. So to get a single *B*-proposition, with a single *B*-truthmaker, we must say *when a* is *F*, as (8) does. And because *F* is a property which *a* may gain or lose at any moment, there are infinitely many such *B*-propositions, all logically independent and all as true (or false) at any one time as at any other. But as nothing in the *B*-sentence '*Fa*' picks out any one of these propositions rather than any other, it has no one *B*-truthmaker, no one *B*-truth-condition and so, in general, no one truth value.

It seems, in other words, as if there is not the *B*-fact *Fa*, located at *t*, which (11) says there is; nor, for the same reason, is there the *B*-fact *F′a*, located at *t′*, which (11′) says there is. The *B*-times *t* and *t′* seem to have to be not *locations* but *constituents* of facts, namely of the facts that *a* is *F* at *t* and *F′* at *t′*. But then it looks as if *F* and *F′* must after all be relations between *a* and times.

A-theorists, by contrast, face no such problem, since '*Fa*', read as an *A*-sentence, always expresses the definite *A*-proposition '*a* is *now F*'. And to prefix this with 'at *t*', whether *t* is a *B*-time like 3.15 or an *A*-time like 'an hour hence', is just to say *when a* is now *F*. So the *A*- or *B*-time *t* in (8) is, as (11) says, the temporal location of the *A*-fact that *a* is now *F*. And it is precisely because this *A*-fact can exist at one time and not at another that (11) does not contradict (11′). *F* need not be a relation to enable *a* to be *now F* at *t* and *not* now *F* at *t′*.

This is why (11), the operator reading of (8), is usually adopted only by *A*-theorists. For to *B*-theorists who wish to deny that *F* is a relation, (11) seems to be no help at all, even if we take '*Fa*' to express the *A*-proposition '*a* is now *F*'. For even on the indexical reading of chapter 6.1, what makes this *A*-proposition true at *t* is still the *B*-fact that *a* is *F* at *t*; and this still makes *F* look like a relation between *a* and *t*.

This I think is why so many *B*-theorists credit even things with temporal parts. Forced to choose, they would rather deny any real distinction between things and events, and hence the reality and temporal nature of change, than admit that changeable properties of things are really relations between things and times.

To me this seems far too high a price to pay to justify the admittedly common conviction that changeable properties are not relations. For on the one hand this common conviction is readily explained by the fact that when, at any *B*-time *t*, we say '*a* is *F*', what we nearly always mean is that *a* is *now* *F*. And even if the *B*-fact that *a* is *F* at *t* is what makes this *A*-statement true, it is not what we *mean*, as we saw in chapter 6.1. Our statement does not express a belief in any relational *B*-proposition, that *a* is *F* at some specific *t*, since we need neither know nor care what that *t* is. The belief that our statement expresses, on the theory of chapter 6.1, is only in a function, from *any t* to its *B*-truth-condition at *t* (that *a* is *F* at *t*), not in the value of this function for some specified *t*. So when '*Fa*' is used to express belief in this function, '*F*' is not even a tacitly relational predicate. It really is, as it seems to be, a one-place predicate applied to *a*. This, I am sure, is why no one thinks of changeable properties as relations, even if they are.

But why then should these properties *not* be relations? For consider how little that would entail about our ascriptions of them: just three things, all of which are clearly true. First, in saying that *a* has a changeable property *F*, it must be said or understood *when a* has *F*, as (8) implies, however it is read. No one will deny that.

Second, since whether a relation links two entities cannot depend on what we call them, (8) cannot depend on how we pick out *a* or *t*. Suppose for example that *a* is the heaviest thing in the room and that *t* is tea-time. Then, if *F* is a relation, it must follow from this and (8) that

> the heaviest thing in the room is *F* at *t*, and
> *a* is *F* at tea-time.

In general: a true '*a* is *F* at *t*' must not be made false by replacing '*a*' or '*t*' with any other name or description of *a* or *t*. That is, both the contexts in

> '... is *F* at ...'

must be what is called *transparent*. And so of course they are.

Third, since nothing can relate what does not exist, if *F* is a relation, (8) must entail the existence of *a* and *t*. This, if less immediately obvious, is also undeniable once three side-issues are disposed of.

The first is fiction. In some sense Hamlet was Gertrude's son despite their not existing, and in that sense 'Hamlet is Gertrude's son' does not entail their existence. On the other hand this proposition was never true in any sense that impugns the Danish census returns that left them out, and that is the only sense which matters here.

The other two issues are whether times can exist without events, and whether, as explained in chapter 5.6, simultaneity across space is relative to reference frames. These are side-issues too, because (8) need entail nothing about either of them in order to entail that *t* exists. The existence of a time like the start of 2020 may or may not depend on there being events 2020 years later than Christ's birth; and temporal locations on *a*'s world line – which is all that *t* and *t′* need to be – need not be simultaneous in every frame with the same parts of the world lines of things far off in space. (8) can entail whatever the existence of *B*-times like *t* may require as easily as it entails the existence of *a*.

Given then that (10) entails nothing false about our ascriptions of *F* to things at times – not even, as we have seen, that '*F*' is a relational predicate – why do so few *B*-theorists accept that changeable properties relate things to times? For that is certainly better than denying the distinction between things and events, and disabling the obvious *B*-theory of change, by taking things as well as events to have temporal parts.

6 The *B*-facts of change

Advocates of temporal-parts may reply to this that, if I can say why our non-relational use of '*F*' in '*a* is now *F*' makes us *think* that *F* is not a relation even if it is, they can say why our *concept* of identity over time makes us distinguish things from events, and change from mere variation, even if there are in reality no such distinctions.

But the two cases are not alike. For while I have shown why we must use '*F*' in '*a* is now *F*' as a non-relational predicate even if *F* is a relation, no one has shown that we must distinguish things from events, and change from spatial variation, even if these distinctions have no basis in reality.

Moreover, even if we had to draw these distinctions, that fact alone can hardly show them to be unreal, any more than our *non*-relational use of '*F*' is what shows *F* to *be* a relation! Such arguments can at best explain why people may be apt to believe something that can be shown on other grounds to be false. But even if no other grounds have yet shown that *F is* a relation, neither has anything I have so far said shown that it is not.

There is however one good reason to prefer (11) to (10) as a reading of (8) and so to deny that *F* and its like are relations. This is that, as I noted at the start of §5, and as (11) says, *t* in (8) is more than an entity to which *a* is related: it is a *location* of *a*. By this I mean that (8) entails that *a* is *at* the time *t*, just as (8′) entails that *a* is *at* the time *t′*: *t* and *t′* are within *a*'s *B*-time. But (10) seems to lack this entailment, since relations generally do not require the entities they link to share locations in space or time. My being *taller than* Napoleon, for example, is quite consistent with his dying before I was conceived; while my conception's being *later than* his death positively requires it.

Still, some relations do entail sameness of temporal location, as – albeit trivially – simultaneity does. But it is no answer to say that changeable properties too are relations which entail this. For what makes (8) entail that *a* is located at *t*, if not the fact that, as I argued in §3, *F*'s being a *non*-relational property requires *a* to be located wherever and whenever *a* is *F*?

I conclude therefore that changeable properties really are, as they seem to be, non-relational properties of things, and that (11), not (10), is the right reading of (8). None of the true entailments of (10) cited at the end of §5 counts against this, since (11) entails them too. That is, (11) also entails that *a* and *t* exist, and lets the truth value of '*Fa*' vary with *t* but not with how *a* and *t* are picked out. For these are still entailments of a relation between *a* and *t*; only now the relation is not *F* but *being located at*.

Yet how, given the arguments of §5, can *B*-theorists accept this reading of (8)? If changeable properties are not relations, must not *B*-theorists conclude that things, like events, have temporal parts? No; and to see why not, we must review the reasons given for this conclusion in §5.

First, I said in §5 that operators like 'at *t*' are supposed to be prefixed to sentences that express definite propositions, i.e. propositions that have, in the relevant circumstances, a definite truth value. But this need not be so. Consider for example the view that there are many possible futures, none of which is yet actual, and the operator 'It is possible that' prefixed to a future-sentence 'P' like 'Jim races tomorrow'. On this view 'It is possible that P' will be true even though 'P' lacks a truth value. Similarly, if for different reasons, 'at *t*, *Fa*' may be true even if '*Fa*' lacks a truth value.

Second, I said that what deprives '*Fa*', read as a *B*-sentence, of a single truth value is that at different times it has different *B*-truthmakers, not all of which exist. That is so, but these *B*-truthmakers need not, as I implied in §5, contain these times as *constituents*, as opposed to having them as their *locations*. In other words, at whatever *B*-times *t* '*Fa*' is true, it can be made true by *B*-facts that differ not in their constituents, *a* and *F*, but only in their locations, *t*.

On this theory the *B*-sentence '*Fa*' will still correspond to infinitely many *B*-truthmakers, one for each *B*-moment *t*. So to give it a unique truth value, something said or understood will have to pick out one of them, as 'at *t*' does. But it need not do this by picking out a truthmaker that has *t* as a constituent: it can do it, as (11) says, by picking out the one and only *Fa* which, if it exists, is located at *t*.

This, I believe, is precisely what 'at *t*' in (8) does: it picks out the *Fa* that is located at *t*. I believe this because it provides the best *B*-theory of change, one that neither makes changeable properties relations nor gives things temporal parts. In this way it lets us admit and explain the distinction between things and events, and hence the existence and temporal nature of change, while requiring things to be, as we know they are, wherever and whenever their changeable properties are.

The only objection I can see to this theory is that it lets many different *B*-facts share all their constituents, such as *a* and *F*. This violates a variant of the so-called 'principle of the identity of indiscernibles', which says that if particulars *a* and *b* share all their properties, then $a=b$. Might we not equally say that if facts Q and R share all their constituents, then Q=R?

Accepting this would make us take *Fa* to be a single fact, whose *B*-time could not then be a moment, or even in general a time interval, since *a* may stop and start being *F* at many different times, which would scatter *Fa* over many disconnected parts of the *B*-time scale. That however is not my main reason for rejecting this otherwise attractive alternative to an infinity of *Fa*-facts. My main reason is a compelling criterion of identity for causal facts to be given in chapter 9.5, namely that such facts are identical if and only if they have the same causes and effects. But then *Fa* cannot be a single fact, since it may, and generally will, have very different causes and effects at different times.

I must therefore deny the identity of many *Fa*-facts. But that is no problem, since I see no more reason to insist on their identity than to deny that many different particulars can share all the properties defined in §3. For an infinity of particulars can obviously share all their non-relational properties, as for example electrons and other fundamental particles can, provided they are differently located in space or time. And if they can, why may not an infinity of different facts share all the same constituents, if they too have different locations in time? I see no reason why not, and so no reason to resist this *B*-theory of change.

7 No experience of the flow of space

In chapter 6.4 I showed how *B*-theorists, while denying that time really flows, can account for our undeniably real, and often true, experiences of time flowing. Now I can use the *B*-theory of change to show why these experiences have no spatial analogue.

This needs showing, since the reason is not at once obvious on a *B*-theory of time. For just as my now-beliefs, like 'It is now 2.15', need to vary from time to time to stay true, so my here-beliefs, like 'Cambridge is here', need to vary from place to place. Yet while, as we saw in chapter 6.4, the first variation makes us experience time as flowing, the second gives us no experience of spatial flow.

To see why not we must first be clear what the right spatial analogue is. It is not changing my here-beliefs to keep them true as I move about; for example, exchanging my belief that Cambridge is here for the belief that London is here when I go to London. This is still only temporal variation. The spatial analogue of changing my now-beliefs to keep them true is this: I am wholly present in two different places s and s' at the same time, at s believing truly that s is here, and at s' believing truly that s' is. This is the spatial analogue we need; and it is of course impossible. Why?

The reason may now seem obvious: nothing that has incompatible properties in different places at the same time is wholly present at either place. A poker that is simultaneously hot at one end and cold at the other is not wholly present at either end. So only some parts of it are hot, and other parts cold: the poker as a whole is neither. That is why, as we saw in §4, this spatial variation is not a change. And similarly with spatial variations in my mental properties. I can have a pain in one foot and not in the other. That difference too is not a change, since I am not wholly present in either foot.

But this is not why my beliefs cannot change spatially. There is an even more basic reason for that, namely that my beliefs, like my shape, are properties of the whole, but not of any part, of me. I cannot, for example, have different beliefs in my two feet, any more than I can have different shapes there, since neither my shape nor my beliefs are properties of my feet. But if I cannot have different here-beliefs in different places at the same time, any more than I can have different shapes, then my here-beliefs, like my shape, can never even *vary* spatially, let alone *change* spatially. That is why there is no spatial analogue of our experience of the flow of time – and this in turn, I believe, is why we never see spatial variation as change.

9 *Events, facts and causation*

1 Events as changes

I have said what change is and what events are, but not how changes are related to events. Yet some relation there must be. If a thing changes, there is an event, and if it does not, there is not. Why is that? Is it because, as many philosophers suppose, events just *are* changes, and can be so defined?

The idea is attractive but for at least two reasons will not do. First, if changes are things having incompatible properties at different times, we may need events to supply the times. Einstein's general theory of relativity admittedly implies that there is more to spacetime than the spatiotemporal relations of things and events, since it explains gravity as an interaction between things and spacetime (their mass affects its curvature, which affects how they move). This may be enough to make spacetime an entity with causal powers (Mellor 1980), but it is not enough to make sense of the idea that everything might have happened, say, ten minutes later than it did, or ten miles to the north. So even in general relativity we may still need events to *identify* points and regions of spacetime and thus particular times. If so, to identify events with changes between times will be circular.

Second, even if all changes are events, not all events are changes. For a start, the beginnings and ends of things need not be changes, since they obviously cannot be changes in *those* things, and need not be changes in anything else. They may be, of course: an animal's death, for example, is usually a change in its body – but not if it is blown to smithereens and its body ends too. Similarly for any thing that is ended by the scattering of its parts. For if the erstwhile parts of a thing cease to interact, they cease to be parts of any whole in the substantial senses of 'part' and 'whole' of chapter 8.2. So even if the parts of a thing *a* survive it, they may not then be parts of anything else at all, let alone of a thing *b* that existed when *a* did and in which *a*'s demise could then have been a change.

Some events too are not even beginnings or ends of things, let alone changes in them, since many are not part of the world line of any thing. Of what thing's world line, for example, is a lightning flash a part? We might I suppose postulate things *ad hoc* for events to be changes in, or even, as a last resort, call them changes in the whole universe. But that is a poor way of making events changes, and no way at all of defining them. And anyway it will not work for the beginning or end (if any) of the universe itself.

In short, if all changes are events, there are more events than changes. But then, far from events being definable as changes, it must if anything be the other way round. Changes must be a species of events. Or must they?

2 Changes: events or facts?

Recall first that I am no longer using 'event' in the broad sense of anything that has (but is not) a time. All I am now calling events are particulars (other than times) that are, unlike things, not wholly present at more than one time. A change, on the other hand, is a thing *a* having incompatible properties *F* and *F′* at different times *t* and *t′*, as in chapter 8.5's

(11) at *t*, *Fa*, and
(11′) at *t′*, *F′a*,

and this makes a change a conjunction of facts, not a particular.

Yet 'change' may mean either, since an argument of Davidson's (1980 essay 6) implies that all the conjunctions I call changes entail corresponding events. To illustrate the argument, suppose that *a* is in Cambridge, *F* and *F′* are temperatures, *F* is much higher than *F′*, and *t′–t* is small, so that

(12) *a* cools quickly in Cambridge;

which obviously entails that

(12a) *a* cools,
(12b) *a* cools quickly, and
(12c) *a* cools in Cambridge.

Yet if it is obvious *that* these entailments hold, it is not obvious *why* they hold – unless (12) entails the existence of a particular which is

(i) a cooling of *a*,
(ii) quick, and
(iii) in Cambridge.

For obviously any particular meeting all the conditions (i)–(iii) must meet any one or two of them: hence the entailments (12a–c). These then, by the so-called 'principle of inference to the best explanation', give us reason to postulate such a particular, which I shall call a *particular change*. For this, if it exists, is surely as entitled to be called the change in *a* as what I shall call the *factual change*, namely the fact that *a* cools.

Similarly in most and perhaps all cases of change. And all particular changes are events, since they all, if not instantaneous, have temporal parts, like *a*'s cooling from *F* to an intermediate temperature, and thence to *F′*.

This account of change meets a major source of scepticism about events, and especially about particular changes. This is that we have so few names for them, as opposed to descriptions using names of things, such as '*a*'s cooling', which could refer as easily to facts (like the fact that *a* cools) as to particulars. We do of course have some names for events, like 'World War II', but far fewer than for things. Yet if there are particular changes, then since most things change often, there must be far more events than things. Why then do we name so few of them?

The reason, I agree with Strawson (1959 chapter 1), is that we use names mainly to reidentify particulars which are wholly present at more than one time and so are what I am calling things. (We may use 'World War II' to refer back to this event at more than one time after it, but that is another matter.) Now while Davidson's theory says that in each case of change *there is* a particular change, it does not thereby *identify* it. And since, being an event, no particular change is wholly present at more than one time, we have no call to *re*identify it, nor therefore to name it in order to do so. This I think is why we usually refer to changes using descriptions, like '*a*'s cooling', which only name the things they are changes in. But if this is why we rarely name changes, we must not infer from their lack of names that they are not particulars.

3 Causes and effects of changes

The case I have so far made for particular changes is, I admit, inconclusive. Nor can I strengthen it by restricting changes to particulars on the grounds that changes have, and therefore are, causes and effects which, as Davidson (1980 essay 7) argues, cannot be facts and so must be particular events. For I think causes and effects include both facts and events. Having argued this fully in chapters 9–12 of *FoC* (*The Facts of Causation*), here I will just sketch the argument, starting with changes, as follows.

Suppose *a* cools over a time interval *t*, with the effect that at a later (but possibly overlapping) interval *t′* a thing *b* (which may or may not be *a*) freezes. Then what I shall call the *factual causation* here is the fact that

(13) *b* freezes because *a* cools, i.e.
the fact that *a* cools causes the fact that *b* freezes.

Now suppose that, as argued in §2, the fact that *a* cools entails that *a*'s world line includes an event, whose *B*-time is *t*, which is a cooling of *a*. Suppose too that the fact that *b* freezes entails that *b*'s world line includes an event, whose *B*-time is *t′*, which is a freezing of *b*. The factual causation is now the fact that, in this region of spacetime,

(14) there is a freezing of *b* because there is a cooling of *a*.

Next, let *c* be the event that is, among other things, the relevant cooling of *a*, and *e* be the event that is, among other things, the relevant freezing of *b*. That is, in the restricted spacetime region relevant to (14),

(15) *c* is the one and only cooling of *a*, and
e is the one and only freezing of *b*.

(14) and (15) I maintain entail that

(16) *c* causes *e*

(or affects it – a distinction that need not concern us here: see chapter 12 of *FoC*). (16) is what I shall call the *particular causation* in this case.

This shows how, if there are particular as well as factual changes, the causation that links the latter will link the former too. Conversely, on the theory of *FoC*, causation will link any particulars *c* and *e* if and only if, for *some* facts *Uc* and *Ve*, there is a *V*-event, namely *e*, because there is a *U*-event, namely *c*. In short, all the particular causes and effects of particular changes correspond to factual causes and effects of corresponding factual changes, and *vice versa*. This is why *B*-theorists of change can be neutral on the question of whether causes and effects are facts or events.

4 The causation of stasis

This neutrality cannot however survive the causation needed to keep things *un*changed. For suppose *a* does *not* cool, but stays *F* from *t* to *t′*, where *t* and *t′* are now *B*-moments. This gives us no such reason as we saw in §2 to postulate a particular other than *a*. To see this, suppose again that *a* is in Cambridge, so that – since *a* cannot cool quickly if it does not cool at all – we have as the analogue of (12) that

(17) *a* does not cool quickly in Cambridge.

Yet (17) entails none of the analogues of (12a–c), namely

(17a) *a* does not cool,
(17b) *a* does not cool quickly, and
(17c) *a* does not cool in Cambridge;

since (17) is consistent with *a*'s cooling slowly in Cambridge, thus making (17a) and (17c) false, or quickly elsewhere, thus making (17b) false.

It cannot therefore be the existence in Cambridge of an event which is a quick non-cooling of *a* that makes (17) a fact; for that would make (17) entail (17a–c), which it does not. On the contrary, all the entailments here go the other way; since

(17a) *a* does not cool

entails that

(17b) *a* does not cool quickly,
(17c) *a* does not cool in Cambridge, and
(17) *a* does not cool quickly in Cambridge.

And the obvious explanation of this is that *no* particular is a cooling of *a*: for if *nothing* is a cooling of *a*, then nothing is either a quick cooling of *a*, or a cooling of *a* in Cambridge, or a quick cooling of *a* in Cambridge.

In short, even if changes are particular events, non-changes cannot be, any more than non-things like *nothing* and *nobody* can be particular things. But then the only particular constituent of *a*'s staying *F* is *a* itself; since for *a* to *stay F* from *t* to *t′* is just for it to *be F* at *t* and *t′* and every moment in between. And as we saw in chapter 8.6, all these logically independent facts have the very same constituents, namely *a* and *F*, being distinguished by having their different times not as constituents but as locations.

Yet there is still causation here. The *Fa*-facts that are located from *t* to *t′* may be *logically* independent, but they are not *causally* independent. It is no coincidence that, if *a* neither absorbs nor emits heat from *t* to *t′*, *a* is *F* at all these times. Nor of course is it an accident that it is *later Fa*s which depend on earlier ones, and not the other way round. The reason is plain: the *Fa*s are causally linked; and causes, as we shall see in chapter 10, must always precede their effects. In short, *a* is *F* at *t′ because* it is *F* at *t*.

But then this causation must be factual, since the *Fa*s it relates contain nothing for particular causation to relate. For *a* is neither caused by nor causes *a*, *t* or *t′*. Nor do *t* and *t′* – which in any case are not constituents of the causally related *Fa*s – cause each other. And there are no other relevant particulars. So in stasis, if not in change, there is no particular causation. The causation it undoubtedly embodies can only be factual.

5 In defence of factual causation

We can therefore no longer keep particular and factual causation on a par. For while all particular causation is derivable from factual causation, as shown in §3, the converse is not true. The fact is that causes and effects are first and foremost facts. Only derivatively, and then only in some cases, do they include particulars.

This fact will prove important in chapter 10 in showing how causation marks off time from space and gives it its direction. Given that, and the still widely accepted objection to factual causation mentioned in §3, I must now summarise the reply to this objection that I give in chapter 9 of *FoC*.

The objection rests on the undeniable fact, invoked in chapter 8.5, that 'whether a relation links two entities cannot depend on what we call them'. So if causation relates the events *c* and *e*, the sentence

(18) '*c* causes *e*'

made true by (16), the fact that *c* causes *e*, cannot be made false by replacing '*c*' or '*e*' with other terms for *c* or *e*. That is, both the contexts in '... causes ...' in (18) must be *transparent*, as indeed they are. Thus if *a*'s cooling is the fastest, and *b*'s freezing is the oddest, event of the day, it follows, if the first event causes the second, that

a's cooling causes the oddest event of the day,
the fastest event of the day causes *b*'s freezing, and
the fastest event of the day causes the oddest one.

Similarly when, in reporting causation using sentences of the form

(19) 'E because C',

where 'C' and 'E' are also sentences like '*a* cools' and '*b* freezes', we treat causes and effects as facts. For as in (13), this is to treat (19) as equivalent to 'The fact that C causes the fact that E', which we may abbreviate to

(20) 'C causes E'

by treating the sentences 'C' and 'E' as names for these facts (if they exist). Then if causation does indeed relate the facts C and E, both the contexts in '... causes ...' should be as transparent in (20) as they are in (18).

Yet they are not. For suppose, to vary the example, that my friend Jim wins his race because he is the fittest man in it, thereby making true all the following equivalent sentences:

(21) 'Jim wins because Jim is the fittest man';
'Jim's is the fastest time because Jim is the fittest man';
'Jim's being the fittest man causes Jim's to be the fastest time'.

But this entails that Jim *is* the fittest man and that Jim's *is* the fastest time. So 'Jim' and 'the fittest man' refer to the same man, and 'Jim's (time)' and 'the fastest time' refer to the same time. So if the contexts in '... causes ...' were transparent in (21), then replacing 'the fittest man' by 'Jim' or 'the fastest time' by 'Jim's (time)', or *vice versa*, would not make (21) false.

Yet it would, because the sentences that would result –

'Jim's being Jim causes Jim's to be the fastest time',
'Jim's being the fittest man causes Jim's time to be Jim's time', etc.

– are all clearly false. It is not because Jim is Jim that he wins his race; his time would be his time however unfit he was; and so on. The fact is that neither context in '... causes ...' is transparent in (21) nor therefore, in general, in (20).

But then it looks as if the causation that (20) reports cannot relate the facts C and E. For if these contexts are opaque – i.e. not transparent – must not (20)'s truth depend on how we refer to C and E, which it could not do if causation related those facts? That is the objection to factual causation.

The reply is simple: (20)'s truth need not and does not depend on how we refer to C and E, because '(the fact that) Jim is the fittest man' and 'Jim is Jim' do not name the same fact; and neither do 'Jim's is the fastest time' and 'Jim's time is Jim's time'. For, as is obvious, the two members of each of these pairs of sentences have completely different truthmakers. Their first members are made true by relational facts (namely Jim's being fitter and faster than all his competitors), and their second members by the mere existence of particulars (Jim and his race, with its time).

The contexts in '... causes ...' need not therefore be transparent in (20) in order for the causation it reports to relate C and E. All (20) needs to do is entail all the sentences got from it by replacing 'C' or 'E' with sentences that *do* name the same facts, which 'Jim is the fittest man' and 'Jim is Jim' do not.

This means however that preserving the identity of the particulars we refer to in sentences like 'Jim is the fittest man' is not always enough to preserve the identity of the facts we thereby state. But then we must ask what more is needed to fix the identity of facts, beyond the identity of the particulars (and properties or relations) we refer to in stating them. What, in short, is our criterion of identity for facts, or at least for those facts that have, and therefore are, causes and effects?

My answer to this question is the same as Davidson's (1980 essay 8) answer to the same question about particular events: *they are identical if and only if they have the same causes and effects*. For Davidson this means that, for any particulars d and d' which have any causes or effects,

$d=d'$ if and only if d and d' have all the same causes and effects.

Or, putting the criterion in linguistic terms, $d=d'$ if and only if for no 'c' or 'e' does replacing 'd' by 'd'' make any true 'c causes d' or 'd causes e' false, or any false one true.

For me it also means that, for any facts D and D′ which have any causes or effects,

D=D′ if and only if D and D′ have all the same causes and effects.

In other words, D=D′ if and only if for no 'C' or 'E' does replacing 'D' by 'D′' make any true 'C causes D' or 'D causes E' false, or any false one true. Or, put in terms of sentences, the fact that D and the fact that D′ are the same fact if and only if for no sentences 'C' or 'E' does replacing 'D' by 'D′' make any true 'E because D' or 'D because C' false, or any false one true.

And if, as I believe, the causal criterion of identity is good enough for causal particulars, it is even better for causal facts. For by making factual causation consistent with opacity in the contexts of '... because ...' it solves a host of problems about all the mental and other causation which requires this opacity. Thus suppose for example I believe truly that my friend Jim is not only the fittest but also the shortest man in his race, because I can see he is. In these circumstances both the sentences

'Jim wins because Jim is the fittest man' and
'I believe Jim is the shortest man, because Jim *is* the shortest man'

are true. Yet of course the sentences

'Jim wins because Jim is the shortest man',
'I believe Jim is the shortest man, because Jim is the fittest man' and
'I believe Jim is the fittest man, because Jim is the shortest man'

are all false; and the reason is obvious. Despite Jim's being both the fittest and the shortest man, those are obviously two different facts about him; just as my believing those two facts are obviously two different facts about me. And by letting all these facts be as different as they evidently are, a causal criterion of identity for facts allows a theory of factual causation to let these facts have – as we can see they do have – quite different physical and mental causes and effects.

10 *Causation and time*

1 Perception, action and time

At the start of chapter 1 I listed the most striking differences between past and future, namely that while we can see (or perceive by other senses) what is past, but cannot affect it, with the future it is the other way round: we can affect but not see it. This does not of course mean that we can see everything that is past or affect everything that is future. What I can see of the past depends on where I am, what I know, what I am looking for and the acuity of my eyes (with or without aids ranging from telescopes to microscopes). What I can affect of the future similarly depends on where I am, what I know, what I can think of doing, and my ability to do it (with or without aids ranging from telephones to rifles). But these constraints are contingent and variable, whereas our inability to see anything in the future or affect anything in the past seems absolute and unchanging. This is so striking a feature of time that any adequate *B*-theory must be able to explain it, and that is not easy.

The difficulty is not that this feature of time is an *A*-feature which is hard to restate in *B*-theory terms. On the contrary, it is easily restatable as follows: at any *B*-time *t*, we can see but not affect what is earlier than *t*, and affect but not see what is later than *t*. This is why I shall feel free in what follows to save words by putting the matter in *A*-terms, referring simply to our inability to see the future or affect the past. When I do so, however, it must be understood that what I mean is the *B*-version of this thesis.

But whichever way we put it, the feature of time that concerns us needs some elaboration and defence before we can explain it. First, I shall take it for granted that we have only one feature here, not two (one to do with action, the other with perception). For all parties agree that the feature in both cases is the same, namely a link between time and causation. With action this is obvious and explicit, since whatever we bring about by our acts or omissions is brought about by causation. The inability of our actions and inactions to affect the past, i.e. to affect anything earlier than them, follows simply from the fact that causes generally precede their effects.

Similarly, if less obviously, with perception. No one denies that to see, hear, smell, feel or taste something is to be affected by it, albeit in very different ways. So what stops our senses showing us the future is the very fact that stops our acts and omissions affecting the past, namely that causes precede their effects. This is the fact to be explained.

Since however some philosophers claim to doubt this fact – or at least its necessity – I must make clear just what, to start with, I am assuming. First, I assume there is no evidence worth discussing that crystal balls or other devices enable the future to be *seen*, as opposed to *fore*seen. I admit of course that we can see facts about the past that justify predictions which we can then make graphic, as in computer-generated images of tomorrow's weather, or planetarium displays of how stars and planets will move across the night sky a million years from now. In this weak sense we can indeed see what is going to happen. But such displays, however well derived by good theories from past perceptions, are still only predictions. They still need to be verified or refuted by real perceptions which, precisely because (for reasons we need not go into) they must be *effects* of what is perceived, will generally occur only after the event.

Second, I shall take it for granted that no science fiction tales of time travellers altering or affecting the actual past provide any evidence at all that this is possible. A more serious case of backward time travel proposed by physicists I shall discuss in chapter 11.1. To start with however I need only assume that at most very few causes are in fact later than their effects. That none are, since none can be, is a conclusion of the ensuing argument, not a premise of it. The premise, which is what the conclusion explains, is the undeniable fact that backward causation is at most very rare.

However, as this is a book about time, what matters here is not what time's link with causation tells us about causation but what it tells us about time. And what, as a *B*-theorist, I think it tells us is how time differs from space, and why that difference makes time the dimension of change, gives it a direction and makes it linear. How the link tells us all this we shall see in due course; but first we need to see what the link is.

2 Causal and temporal order

The fact that most if not all causes and effects are separated in time already marks a difference between time and space that needs explaining, since the fact has no spatial analogue. Causes and effects are often in the same place, as when the unchanging thing *a* of chapter 9.4 is also unmoving. And when an effect is not where its causes are, it may be north or south, west or east, above or below them. The cause–effect relation has no preferred spatial direction. Why then does it have a temporal one?

There are *A*-theory answers to this question which, having rejected the *A*-theory on other grounds, I shall not discuss. The question for us is how *B*-theorists can explain the correlation between causal and temporal order. The answer is that we cannot unless we take the latter to be entailed by the former. For if we take these two orders to be independent, it should be as conceivable that effects generally precede their causes as that causes generally precede their effects. Yet not even those who think that some causes may be later than their effects think that all or even most could be.

But then may not the dependence between the earlier–later and cause–effect relations go the other way? Why, in particular, may we not *define* a cause as the earlier of two causally related facts or events? The answer is that there are at least two other ways of distinguishing causes from effects, with which this definition could then conflict. These follow from the fact that whereas causes both *explain* their effects and provide *means* of bringing them about, effects neither explain nor provide means of bringing about their causes.

Take the example in chapter 9.5 of Jim winning his race because he is the fittest man in it. The cause here is Jim's comparative fitness before the race, and the effect is that he wins. This, I argue in chapters 5.4 and 7.1 of *FoC* (*The Facts of Causation*), implies that Jim's fitness both explains his winning and is a means to it. And so of course it does and is: indeed it was to get a means of winning the race that Jim made himself fit in advance. Yet clearly the converse is not true: Jim's winning the race neither explains nor is a means to his earlier fitness. And similarly in all other cases.

Either of these links, between causing something, and explaining and being a means to it, could thus be used to define a cause as that one of two causally related facts which explains or is a means to the other. But then we must ask why these two definitions pick out the same member of each pair of causally related facts, and no definition will tell us that. Similarly, defining a cause as the earlier member of any cause–effect pair only prompts the query: why does this definition select the same causes as the other two definitions, a question which again no definition can answer.

My own answer to these questions, given in chapters 6 and 7 of *FoC*, is that every cause must raise the chances of its effects. This I argue is what makes a cause like Jim's fitness explain and be a means to its effects, like his winning his race: his being fit makes his chance of winning greater than it would have been had he been less fit. And a consequence of this condition is also what makes time linear, as we shall see in chapter 12.

This claim, that causes must raise their effects' chances, is unfortunately still too contentious for me to take it for granted here. But I do not need to. All I need here is the fact that we cannot reduce the causal order of facts and events to their temporal order, and that is undeniable. The mere fact that Jim wins his race *after* he gets fit will obviously not tell us what makes his getting fit explain and be a means to, and hence be a cause rather than an effect of, his winning.

So if the general coincidence of causal and temporal order is to be more than a coincidence, it cannot be because time order fixes causal order. It must be the other way round.

3 Simultaneous causation

But what then of the many cases where causation seems to be simultaneous? Kant (1781 A203) even thought that 'the great majority of efficient natural causes are simultaneous with their effects', giving his famous and plausible example where

> if I view as a cause a ball which impresses a hollow as it lies on a stuffed cushion, the cause is simultaneous with the effect.

Why should we deny this?

We have several incentives to deny it. First, however many causes and effects are simultaneous, we still have to explain why the causal order of those that are not simultaneous is correlated with their time order when it is correlated with no spatial order, and there is no credible explanation of this difference that lets any causation be simultaneous.

Second, causation is the obvious basis of the distinction of timelike from spacelike intervals in relativity explained in chapter 5.5. We saw in chapter 9.4 how a thing *a*'s having a property *F* at a time *t* can cause it to remain *F* until a later time *t′*. So if *a* moves from a place *s* at *t* to a place *s′* at *t′*, then whatever causes *a* to be *F* at *s* can be an indirect cause of whatever its being *F* at *s′* causes. This is how moving things transmit causation across space, as when light made red by reflection from Mars causes us to see that Mars is red. This, together with the fact that in special relativity no thing can be made to go faster than light, suggests that light is the fastest transmitter of causation, and thus that no facts or events whose separation is spacelike can be related as cause to effect. But then in no reference frame can causation at any distance, however small, be simultaneous.

This is admittedly denied in theories which postulate action at a spatial distance that is unmediated, or mediated by so-called *tachyons* that always travel faster than light, which relativity allows. But the only evidence for such action is the so-called *nonlocality* of quantum theory, which threatens not the contiguity of causation but only something weaker, namely 'the sense of locality that requires that correlation between spacelike separated events always be factorable-out by a common cause' (Skyrms 1980 p. 127).

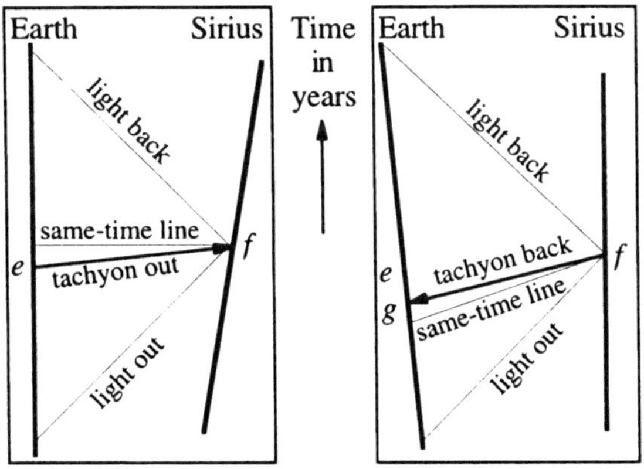

Figure 8

Moreover, if causes did have effects separated from them by spacelike intervals, they would also have absolutely earlier effects, i.e. effects earlier than them in all reference frames. For then, as shown in Figure 8 (adapted from Figure 1 of chapter 1.4), a tachyon which transmitted causation could leave earth (*e*), be reflected from Sirius (*f*) and return to earth (*g*) before it leaves. In short, if in relativity causes and effects could have spacelike separations, and so be simultaneous in some reference frame, causes could be absolutely later than their effects. But that they cannot be, as we shall see in chapter 12.

Finally, simultaneous causation conflicts with what Le Poidevin (1991 chapter 6) calls 'reciprocity' laws, like Newton's third law of motion, which says that the momentum of each of two colliding things causes the other's momentum to change. If these causes and effects were simultaneous, this would make each thing have its changed and unchanged momentum at the same time, which is obviously impossible.

These objections give us every reason to try and explain away apparent examples of simultaneous causation, encouraged by Kant's statement that even in his cushion case he will still distinguish cause and effect by 'the time relation of their dynamical connection', thus illustrating his earlier conclusion that even though

> the time between ... the cause and its immediate effect may be a vanishing quantity, and they may thus be simultaneous ... the relation of the one to the other will always still remain determinable in time (Kant 1781 A203).

To see what that means in this case, suppose first that Kant's cushion is elastic, so that removing the ball will make it lose its hollow. But not of course until *after* the ball is removed. But then what the ball's lying there at any *B*-moment *t* causes is the hollow not *at* but just *after t*. While if the cushion is *in*elastic, and would keep its hollow anyway, then, as with other unchanging things, what causes it to have a hollow at *t* is its having a hollow just *before t*. So in neither case is the causation simultaneous except in Kant's false sense (in the last quotation) that the cause precedes its effect by a vanishingly small time. But that still makes it earlier than its effect, and so not simultaneous with it in any sense that matters here.

But what about the ball's initial impact on the cushion? Its hollow cannot form *after* the impact, or the ball would not be on but *in* the cushion, which clearly it is not, and certainly need not be. But then must not this causation be simultaneous? No: but to see why not, we must first deal with another apparent case of simultaneous causation.

Imagine a rigid rear-engined train moving off. If it is perfectly rigid, it cannot contract. Yet it must, if its rear moves off before its front. So the whole train must move as one: the front's movement must be simultaneous with that of the engine at the rear which causes it.

To this I reply that nothing can be *perfectly* rigid in this sense. Yet there need be no limit to how close to perfect rigidity a thing can get. This follows from the density of space and time, which prevents any spacetime point being next to any other. So suppose the train's rear moves off at a moment *t* and its front at a later moment *t′*. Then however long the train, and however small *t′–t*, there are infinitely many moments between *t* and *t′* at which points on the train can all move off in turn.

Similarly with the impact of Kant's ball on his cushion. The cushion's inevitably imperfect rigidity lets every point within it start to move only *after* the surface between it and the ball starts to move.

Other apparent cases of simultaneous causation are provided by fields: electrical, gravitational, etc. Take for example a point particle *q* whose electric charge *E* at a spacetime point *st* makes it affect the electrostatic field at all points absolutely later than *st*. Yet how can it do this without affecting the field at *st* where this *Eq*-fact is, i.e. without a simultaneous effect? For would that not imply unmediated action at a distance?

No, again because of the density of space and time. This, by stopping any other spacetime point being next to *st*, makes *all* this *Eq*-fact's effects at other points, however close, be at a distance. But then it also lets its effect at any such point be mediated by its effects at intermediate points. So while all the later action here must be at a distance, it can also all be mediated. This is why, in a dense spacetime, the *Eq*-fact at *st* need only affect the electrostatic field at all points later than *st*. It need not affect the field where it itself is, and so need not entail any simultaneous causation.

What, finally, of Newton's theory of gravity, which says that all things exert gravitational forces on all other things, however far away? Does this not imply unmediated action at a distance? No, for as Newton (1713 book III, general scholium) says, although by his theory

> we have explained the phenomena of the heavens and of our sea by the power of gravity, [we] have not yet assigned the cause of this power. ... Hitherto I have not been able to discover the cause of those properties of gravity ... and I frame no hypotheses.

But nothing in Newton's theory rules out hypotheses, e.g. that gravity is mediated by a field, which do not require unmediated action at a distance. Nor does it demand simultaneous causation, as we can see by comparing the gravitational field between two things to the carriages linking a train's engine to the other end of the train that it causes to move.

4 Ordering facts, events and times

I conclude from all this that we need not reject an otherwise acceptable *B*-theory of why most causes precede their effects just because it entails that they all do, thus ruling out simultaneous causation. But why then should we not adopt the most obvious way of making causation do this, by *defining* time order as causal order?

One obvious reason is that so few temporally ordered facts and events are causally related. The causes and effects of any such fact or event will include only the minutest fraction of all the world's earlier and later facts or events, even on the contentious assumption that causation is transitive, i.e. that the effects of every cause automatically include all the effects of its effects, all their effects, and so on without end.

Yet the shortage of causally related facts and events does not in fact stop us reducing time order to causal order. To show why not, I must first say what I mean by the time order of *facts*, since usually only particulars, like events and times, are said to be earlier or later than each other. I think the reason for this is that while, for events *c* and *e*, the temporal analogue of

(18) '*c* causes *e*', namely
(22) '*c* precedes *e*',

is obvious, it is less obvious that the temporal analogue of

(19) 'E because C', namely
(23) 'E after C'

(e.g. 'Jim wins his race after he gets fit'), entails the temporal analogue of

(20) 'C causes E', namely
(24) 'C precedes E',

(e.g. 'Jim's getting fit precedes his winning his race').

Yet this *is* entailed, because (23), like (19), entails both 'C' and 'E': Jim cannot win his race after he gets fit unless he both gets fit and wins his race. This means that we can always restate (23) as 'The fact that C precedes the fact that E', and then abbreviate this to (24). The parallel with causation is complete. So in particular, if '*c* causes *e*' entails '*c* precedes *e*' for all *c* and *e*, 'C causes E' can also entail 'C precedes E' for all C and E.

However, even these contentious entailments still seem too few to serve our turn. For they do not alter the fact that (22), (23) and (24) have many more true instances than their causal counterparts do. How then, when an event *c* or a fact C precedes an event *e* or a fact E which it does *not* cause, can the time order of these events or facts follow from some causal order?

The answer lies in an important difference between events and times. To see this difference we must first generalise the example I used in chapter 9.3 to show how (18) can follow from (19). As that example suggests, (18) will follow from (19) whenever C and E are existential facts about events: for then (19) will entail that, in a suitably restricted region of spacetime, and for some properties *F* and *G* of events,

(25) there is a *G*-event *because* there is an *F*-event, and hence that
(26) there is a *G*-event *after* there is an *F*-event.

Next, as in chapter 9.3, (25) and (26) entail that, in the relevant region,

(27) the *F*-event *causes* (or affects) the *G*-event, and
(28) the *F*-event *precedes* the *G*-event.

Then the difference between events and times is this: whereas not all causally and hence temporally related facts C and E are existential facts about events, they *are* all existential facts about *B*-times. For this just means that all such facts *have* moments or intervals of time as their temporal locations. This being so, *every*

(24) 'C precedes E' entails that
(29) C's *B*-time *t* precedes E's *B*-time *t′*

(where if they are intervals *t* and *t′* may overlap, provided *t′* includes some moments later but none earlier than *t*).

In other words, C's *B*-time precedes E's because C precedes E, not the other way round. And just as I said in chapter 9.3 that, on the theory of

FoC, *c* causes *e* if and only if, for *some* facts *Uc* and *Ve*, there is a *V*-event, *e*, because there is a *U*-event, *c*, so I say now that for all *B*-times *t* and *t′*,

t precedes *t′*

if and only if, for *some* facts Q and R which are not just about times and their temporal relations,

t is Q's *B*-time, *t′* is R's *B*-time and Q precedes R;

and similarly for *B*-places, spacetime points and regions. This is why in chapter 9.1 I said, following Leibniz, that the idea that everything might have happened ten minutes later than it actually does makes no sense. The existence and identities of times derive in the end from the existence and time order of facts about other things.

Yet the existence of times still enables us, despite the apparent shortage of causally related facts, to derive all time order from causal order. For each point of spacetime is the location of many facts, e.g. about density, curvature, pressure, temperature, the intensity of gravitational, electromagnetic and other fields, etc., all of them related causally to *some* other facts at other points. So all we need, for causation to fix the time order of any two spacetime points, and hence of *t* and *t′*, is – in this case – that *some* fact C at *t* causes *some* fact E at *t′*, thereby making all other facts at *t* also precede all other facts at *t′*, whether they cause those later facts or not.

This shows how the time order of all facts can follow from the causal order of some of them. But it faces an immediate objection. For if C at *t* can cause E at *t′*, a fact Q at *t′* should be able to cause a fact R at *t*. Yet it cannot, the objection runs, because that would make *t* both earlier and later than *t′*, which is a contradiction. But this objection runs too fast, since it is not obvious that being both earlier and later than something, as opposed to being both earlier and *not* earlier than it, *is* a contradiction. Certainly nothing I have said so far shows that it is.

For example, I have not yet shown why a time machine like Dr Who's TARDIS cannot leave at *t′* and arrive – later – at an earlier *t*, thus making *t′* both earlier and later than *t*; nor why time itself cannot be circular, thus making *all* times both earlier and later than all other times. In chapter 12 I will indeed show why this cannot happen, by showing why causal loops (which a causal basis for time order makes these timelike loops entail) are impossible. But until then the apparent possibility of timelike loops, and hence of backward causation, is no obstacle to a reduction of time order to causal order. On the contrary, it meets the other common objection to any such reduction, namely that it would rule out backward causation by mere definition. If that is an objection, then the fact that our reduction does no such thing – since it just makes backward causation entail a locally reversed time order – is not a defect but a merit.

5 The causal form of inner sense

Yet even if a reduction of temporal to causal order allows some backward causation, the reduction can still not be done by *definition*. The obstacle here lies in our ability, stressed in chapter 1.5, to perceive the time order of many facts and events. This ability rests in turn on the fact that not only our perceptions but all our experiences have a time order that we directly perceive. Thus if, to revive the example of chapter 1.5, I see a clock hand pass '1' before it passes '2', I know that I do, and similarly for other experiences: their time order is self-intimating. But then we could use this fact, as Kant does, to define time as 'nothing but the form of inner sense' (1781 B50), meaning that it is the dimension of our experiences, thus defining time order as the self-intimating order of these experiences.

But this definition will not do, because it does not explain why causes precede their effects. Equally, defining time order as causal order does not explain how we know the time order, so defined, of our experiences. The question again, as in §2, is why two appealing but seemingly independent definitions of the same thing give the same result, and no definition will tell us that. What will tell us that is the following causal theory of how we see time order, first in external events and facts, and then in our experiences.

Suppose I see two external events *e* and *f*, like my clock hand passing '1' and '2', and let *pe* and *pf* be my perceptions of them. Suppose too that by seeing *e* and *f* I see also that *e* precedes *f*. (We need not assume that *e does* precede *f*, nor even that I believe it does, since I may not trust my senses in this case, as I do not when they tell me that lightning precedes thunder: what matters here is what my senses tell me, not whether I believe them, or whether they are right.) Next, since it is obvious that I need no experiences other than *pe* and *pf* to see in this way that *e* precedes *f*, we may suppose that nothing else does make me see this. Yet even so there must be more to my seeing *e* precede *f* than my seeing *e* and seeing *f*, since I could see *e* and *f* and either not see their time order at all or see instead that *f* precedes *e*. What, if not a third experience, makes the difference?

The answer could lie, as Dennett (1991 chapter 6.3) says, in unconscious visual processing, driven perhaps by induction from the usual time order of events like *e* and *f*, e.g. the fact that most clock hands pass '1' before '2'. But again this need not be so, and I will assume that it is not so. But then it seems that the answer must lie in the time order of *pe* and *pf*. When I see *e* precede *f*, I do so because I see *e before* I see *f*, i.e. because *pe* precedes *pf*. Had I seen *f* first, i.e. had *pf* preceded *pe*, I would have seen *f* precede *e*.

Yet this is still not quite right, since it does not explain why my eyes tell me anything at all about the order of *e* and *f*. For me to see *e* precede *f*, it is not enough for me to see *e* and *f* and see *e* first: when I see *f* I must also, in some weak sense, *remember* seeing *e*. For clearly I cannot see *e* precede *f* until I see *f*, and can only do so then if my seeing *e* has left some trace in me. In other words, for me to see *e* precede *f* just by seeing *e* and *f*, *pe* must *affect pf* in some way such that, had *pf* affected *pe* in that way, I would have seen *f* precede *e*.

This gives us the answer we need. For if *pe* affects *pf*, and causal order entails temporal order, then *pe must* precede *pf*; and similarly the other way round: if *pf* affects *pe*, it must also precede *pe*. In short, the causal order of *pe* and *pf* fixes both the time order that these perceptions of *e* and *f* have and the time order that they make me perceive *e* and *f* to have.

This is why the time order of our perceptions of events and facts almost always coincides with the time order which they make us perceive those events and facts to have. Yet of course, as the lightning and thunder case shows, that order may not coincide with the time order of the events or facts themselves – unless those events or facts are also experiences of ours. For if our own experiences, unlike lightning and thunder, all take the same short time to intimate themselves to us, their time order must be that of our perceptions of them. But then, since this will also be, as we have just seen, the time order we thereby perceive those experiences to have, our perceptions of that time order must be right.

This is how causation gives us the all but infallible knowledge of the time order of our own experiences that makes Kant's definition of time so appealing. It is because causation does this that time's being, as I say it is, the causal dimension of spacetime makes it also, as Kant says it is, the form – the causal form – of inner sense.

6 Causation and change

Now we know how causation distinguishes time from space, we can answer a question left over from chapter 8. How does time's being the causal dimension of spacetime explain why only temporal variation is change?

To answer this question we must first recall the theory of change given in chapter 8. Variation occurs when incompatible properties, like different temperatures, which no particular can have in the same place at the same time, are had at different points or regions of spacetime. This variation can be change only if it is more than different particulars having different properties, since all parties agree that change needs identity as well as difference. Your being hot and my being cold is not a change, since in this case no one particular changes. Our thermal variation is only a difference between us: you are hot, I am cold, and that is all there is to it. Nor would our being parts of something else, like a pantomime horse, make this variation change, for it would not make the horse as a whole either hot or cold, let alone both. And as with the horse, so with every spatially extended thing or event. No spatial variation across it is a change, since none is more than a difference between different spatial parts of the whole particular.

Similarly, no variation over time in any *event* is a change, since it is only ever a difference between different parts of that event. In a person, animal or other *thing*, however, a temporal variation *is* a change: for since a thing has no temporal parts, its varying properties are all properties of a single particular, in which they can therefore be changes. This then is my *B*-theory of what change is: temporal variation in the properties of things. And the question that the theory poses now is this: how does time's being the causal dimension of spacetime enable particulars whose properties vary over time and space to lack temporal but not spatial parts? How, in other words, does causation enable things to be wholly present at different times but not (at the same time) at different places?

The answer lies in how the existence and identities of particulars located in space and time depend on their properties. Some of my properties may be essential to me, i.e. such that without them I would not exist. Perhaps my being human is such a property: perhaps nothing could be me that was not human. My precise *B*-time, on the other hand, is clearly an inessential property, since my life could well be slightly shorter or longer than it will be. What then makes a property essential to people, or to particulars of other kinds? This is a hard question, and may indeed have no answer, since there may well be no distinction of kind between essential and inessential properties. That is, it may be that all a particular needs in order to exist in other possible worlds is *enough* of the properties it has in this one (or enough at least of those we care about, like the many properties that go to make us human).

This however is not a question we need to answer. For what we need to start with is a different if related question, namely what apparently *changeable* properties are essential to a thing's *survival*, i.e. are such that losing them would be the end of it? That this is a different question is not always realised, and often does not matter; but here it does, since it may have relevantly different answers. For even if nothing that is never human could be me, I might still be able to *change* into, say, a rhinoceros – provided I change slowly, with enough intermediate stages and, perhaps, without ever losing some so-called *sortal* property (Wiggins 1980 chapters 2–3), like being an animal.

These provisos hold the key. All parties agree that, even if a thing could change all its properties one at a time, it must still, while changing any one of them, keep some (or enough) other properties to preserve its identity through that change. So suppose a thing *a* changes from being *G* at *t* to being *G′* at a slightly later *t′*. For *a* to survive this change – and hence for this to *be* a change in *a* – some of *a*'s other properties *F* must be *un*changed from *t* to *t′*. And as we saw in chapter 9.4, what keeps any property of *a* unchanged is causation: *a* is *F* at *t′ because* it is *F* at *t*. So for *a* to change from being *G* at *t* to being *G′* at *t′*, causation must link some other facts about it at those two times.

This is why change has no spatial counterpart. Because causation cannot link facts across spacelike intervals, it cannot yield the spatial constancy needed to make different properties of a thing's spatial parts properties of a single particular. This in turn is why spatial variations of density, hardness, conductivity, composition, colour, etc., within a thing may be, and usually are, far more abrupt and discontinuous than temporal variations of those properties in that thing. It is why, in the extreme case, a thing's spatial parts may even be separated in space (as I noted in chapter 8.2 that the gas particles postulated by kinetic theory are), just as an event's temporal parts (e.g. the courses of a meal or the acts of a play) may be separated in time. For neither needs the continuous possession of properties that is required to preserve a thing's identity through a single change, which is what stops the *B*-times of things being discontinuous. All this is explained, and only explained, by the fact that time is the causal dimension of spacetime.

11 *The direction of time*

1 Earlier and later

The direction of time is the difference between being *earlier* than something and being *later* than it. The difference is not formal, as these relations are not differently related to each other: each is just the other's converse. That is, any fact C is by definition earlier than any other fact D if and only if D is later than C (and similarly of course for events and things). Nor do these relations have different formal properties: both are (i) transitive, (ii) asymmetric and (iii) irreflexive. That is, for all C, D and E:

(i) if C is earlier (later) than D and D is earlier (later) than E, then C is earlier (later) than E;
(ii) if C is earlier (later) than D, D is not earlier (later) than C;
(iii) C is neither earlier nor later than itself.

((ii) and (iii) assume that, as we shall see, there are no timelike loops of the sort described in chapter 10.4. If there were, (ii) and (iii) would be false: if for example time was circular every fact would be both earlier and later than every other fact, including itself. But even then earlier and later would not differ formally, since each would be symmetrical and reflexive.)

What then *is* the direction of time: how *do* earlier and later differ? The answer is that they differ in their consequences, notably the consequences for perception and action noted in chapter 10.1. When I am earlier than a fact which I can affect I cannot perceive it, and when I am later than a fact which I can perceive I cannot affect it. And all these differences reduce as we have seen to a single causal difference, the fact that causes precede their effects. Hence the causal theory of time order, which makes (ii) and (iii), the asymmetry and irreflexivity of earlier and later, follow from the fact, yet to be proved, that nothing can cause or affect either itself or its causes. It also tells us why the direction of time has no spatial analogue, since as I noted in chapter 10.2, causes have effects in all spatial directions

But how does the causal theory explain (i), the transitivity of earlier and later? If, as many hold, causation itself is transitive, so that if C causes D and D causes E, it follows that C causes E, there is of course no problem.

But this is a contentious thesis, which I reject because it deprives causation of key implications, like those cited in chapter 10.2, namely that causes *explain* and are *means* to their effects. For if, as I hold, these consequences of causation are not transitive, causation cannot be transitive either.

However for present purposes it does not matter whether causation is transitive, which is why I need not argue the point here. For even if it is not, it can still entail an earlier–later relation that is, via its so-called *ancestral*, the self-evidently transitive relation that holds between C and E if and only if C is a causal *ancestor* of E, i.e. if and only if C causes E, or causes a D that causes E, or causes a D that causes a D′ that causes E, or ....

Yet for all its obvious virtues, the causal theory is not the only *B*-theory of the direction of time. It has at least three rivals, each based on one of the three general facts that

(a) the universe is expanding,
(b) the entropy of isolated systems increases, and
(c) radiation expands outwards from its sources.

But although (a)–(c) have all been thought to generate, and used to define, the direction of time, it should be obvious that none of them will do the job. For a start, none of them explains our natural ability to *perceive* time order, as we saw in chapter 10.5 that the causal theory does. Nor does any of them tell us why causes generally precede their effects, nor therefore why we cannot see the future or affect the past. And as *definitions* of time order, they all have absurd entailments: namely that (a) in no circumstances could the universe cease to expand, when clearly it could; (b) the entropy of an isolated system could never decrease, or even stay constant, which it often does; and (c) radiation could never converge, which any convex lens or concave mirror can make it do.

Why then have such incredible definitions been proposed? The reason is a supposed connection between the direction of time and what are called *irreversible processes*. These are processes in which events or facts of asymmetrically related kinds always or mostly occur in only one time order. Thus most isolated systems have lower entropies, and most clusters of photons – and all expanding universes – have smaller volumes, at earlier times than at later ones. But why is this so: why are these and other processes irreversible in this sense, given that theories of, say, classical mechanics do not require them to be so? Suppose for example you reverse a video of me cleaning a blackboard: the process it will then depict, of me *un*cleaning the board, is just as consistent with classical mechanics as is my cleaning of it. Why then does such uncleaning never happen: why does reversing the path of my board duster never restore the words it has just wiped off?

The short answer is of course that it takes more than classical mechanics to explain irreversible processes. Why should it not? Why must all laws let events or facts of distinct kinds F and G, like smaller and larger volumes, or lower and higher entropies, follow each other in either order (or, in the case of statistical laws, give them significant chances of doing so)? I can see no good answer to this question, and hence no reason to be puzzled by the fact that some laws let processes be reversible and others do not.

There is indeed more to be said about what makes processes irreversible in this sense; but not here, since irreversibility has nothing to do with what gives time its direction. The fact is that the direction of time does not depend on the existence of irreversible processes. But given the widespread belief that it does, which is the basic mistake that motivates definitions based on (a)–(c), I must now say why it does not.

First, let us call processes that link events with incompatible properties F and G 'FG-processes' and divide them into F-processes, where F-events precede G-events, and G-processes, where G-events precede F-events. Then FG-processes are reversible if processes of both F- and G-types occur, and irreversible if only F- or only G-processes occur.

An example of an FG-process is our clock hand of chapter 1.5 moving past '1' (an F-event) and '2' (a G-event) in a single circuit starting at '12'. Let us call the clock c. Then these processes in c are irreversible, since c's hands always move one way, so that F-events always precede G-events. So suppose we use this fact to define the direction of time, as that from F-events to G-events, i.e. from a clock hand's passing '1' to its passing '2'. Then if ever the time order of events of these kinds seems reversed, i.e. if a clock hand seems to move anti-clockwise, as it would if a clock – call it c' – were travelling back in time, we must take this to be a local reversal of the direction of time. And so indeed we would in that case.

But not in the case of a clock c'' whose hands are *made* to move anti-clockwise: so there must be more to backward time travel than that. But what more? How must c'' differ from c'? The answer is that its *clockwork* must differ. c and c' have the same clockwork, the same causal mechanism, which makes their FG-processes irreversible by letting F-events affect G-events but not *vice versa*. Thus, on either c or c', bending the hand as it passes '1' will make it bent as it passes '2', but not *vice versa*. Whereas on c'', where the causal order of F- and G-events is reversed, bending the hand as it passes '1' will *not* make it bent as it passes '2'. All this is shown in Figure 9.

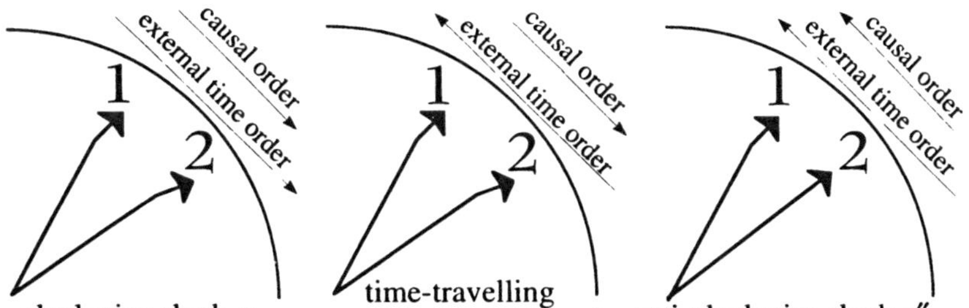

Figure 9

What Figure 9 shows is that, as our causal theory of time order asserts, reversing the direction of time means reversing the time order of *token* causes and effects, as the time-travelling clock c' does. Reversing the normal time order of events or facts of different *types*, like F and G, as the anti-clockwise clock c'' does, is irrelevant. But then it is irrelevant whether there *is* a normal time order of types of events or facts, i.e. whether any processes are irreversible. This is why the direction of time does not need, and cannot be defined by, any irreversible processes, neither those of (a)–(c) nor any others.

Failure to see the irrelevance of irreversibility shows up not only in definitions of time's direction based on (a)–(c) but also in the idea, once-fashionable, that positrons are electrons travelling backward in time. To get this idea suppose the negative charge of an electron e draws it towards a positive charge +, i.e. makes it nearer to + at later times than at earlier ones. The charge on an electron e' travelling back in time will then make e' nearer to + at what to us are *earlier* times, and so make + seem to repel it – just as it repels the positively charged positron e''. Hence the idea that e'' just *is* a time-travelling electron.

But it is not, any more than an anti-clockwise clock is a time-travelling clockwise clock, and for the same reason. For e'' to be like c' rather than c'', the causal order of facts about it would have to be reversed, so that (e.g.) where e'' is at any moment depended on where it is at our *later* times. But of course it does not. The causal and our time orders of facts coincide in positrons just as they do in anti-clockwise clocks. So if the latter are not travelling back in time, neither are the former, as Figure 10 shows. Here again we see that what gives time its direction is not an irreversible process – in this case negative and positive charges moving closer to each other – but the direction of causation, i.e. the asymmetry of the cause–effect relation.

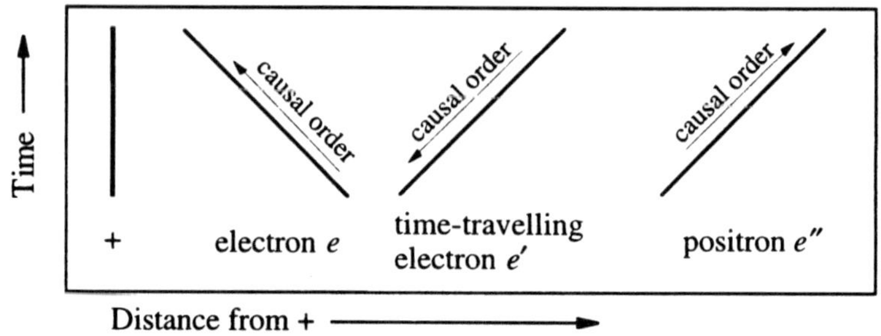

Figure 10

2 Experiencing the direction of time

So much for the direction of time. What of our experience of it? In chapter 6.4 I showed how we experience the flow of time by constantly changing our *A*-beliefs, and especially our beliefs about what is happening *now*, in order to keep them true. But this does not explain the *direction* of that experience, i.e. why the flow of time seems to take us forward into the future rather than backward into the past. What does that is the causation that gives us our cumulative memories.

To recall something that I have perceived is in effect to perceive it again via my original perception. So as a kind of indirect perception, recollection has its own causal mechanism, that of memory. Suppose for example I recall an event *e* that I have seen. To enable me to do this, my perception *pe* of *e* must leave a trace in me, like the trace which I said in chapter 10.5 enables my later perception *pf* of another event *f* to tell me that *e* precedes *f*, i.e. that *f* succeeds *e*. Indeed my seeing in this way that *f* succeeds *e* is just a special case of recalling *e*.

Suppose now that I see a third event *g* and thereby, through the causal mechanism of chapter 10.5, that *g* succeeds *f*. This mechanism requires my perception *pg* of *g* to be affected by my perception *pf* of *f*, and the effect on *pg* may also be such as to make it incorporate a recollection not only of *f* but of *f* succeeding *e*.

Similarly, my seeing a fourth event *h* succeeding *g* may incorporate recollections of first *f* and then *g* succeeding *e*. And so on indefinitely. If I successively see these events succeeding each other, I may thereby recall *e*'s being succeeded by ever more events, which I may also recall succeeding one another. This will make me recall an increasingly long chain of events between *e* and whatever I am currently perceiving. This I believe is what makes the flow of time seem to take me further and further from any event or fact I perceive, as later perceptions keep adding to the events and facts that I can recall succeeding both it and each other.

The way in which the flow of time appears to take us toward the upshots of our actions is a special case of this process. Seeing if an action of mine succeeds means seeing if it has the upshot I recall intending it to have when I did it. The causal mechanisms of action and perception then fix the time order of these events or facts as follows: first my intention, then my action, then its upshot and then my perception of its upshot. My accumulating recollections of events and facts will thus include my recollections of members of such sequences, acquired in this order, which will therefore be the order in which the flow of time appears to take me through them.

Similarly for the simpler special case of checking a prediction. Seeing if a prediction of mine succeeds means seeing if the fact I predict actually exists. This fact may not be the upshot of an action of mine, but my seeing it will be, if only the upshot of my looking for it. So again the causal order of the members of this sequence will fix their time order as follows: prediction, action, perception. And as each member of the sequence will be a change in me, which I can recall simultaneously with my perceptions of later but not of earlier members, this too will be the order in which the flow of time appears to take me through them.

Finally, as for the causal sequence of events or facts involved in one action, so for sequences of actions, including causal sequences constituting larger actions, like the sequence of steps that takes me out of a room. As I see the intended upshot of each attempted step, that action is added to my accumulating store of recollectable past events, and so the perceived flow of time will take me successively through the sequence from each step to its causal and hence its temporal descendant.

In short, our experience of the direction of time demands nothing more than an accumulation of memories, of memories of memories, and so on. This, and the fact that memories are effects of what we remember, is what, on a causal theory of time order, makes the flow of time seem to take us forward into the future rather than back into the past.

3 Forward time travel

Our having this experience of travelling into the future does not of course show that we can travel in time in any more objective sense. Yet in fact we can, as even *B*-theorists can admit.

Real forward time travel, unlike the apparent flow of time, is more than psychological, and is not restricted to the latter's tautological rate of seven days a week. An example of it would be someone taking only an hour to reach the end of the next century, and that in principle can be done.

Admittedly much science fiction makes time travellers vanish during such journeys, thus giving them a discontinuous *B*-time, which for reasons given in §1 they cannot have. But that is only a melodramatic embellishment and by no means essential to the story. And apart from that, all forward time travellers need do is reduce their rates of change and decay so much that they take a century to reach physical and mental states which they would otherwise reach in an hour, and there are at least two ways of doing that.

One is provided by special relativity, and will work for anything: just send it off in an extremely fast spaceship that will return to earth a hundred earth years later. The spaceship and its contents will then have aged – in the serious *B*-theory sense of chapter 8.3 – much less than similar things and processes on earth, the discrepancy increasing with the spaceship's speed. If it sets off in AD 2000 at a speed close enough to that of light, then it and its contents will have aged no more than an hour when it returns in AD 2100. That is, the spaceship's clocks, people, things and processes of all kinds will on its return be in the states which they would have reached on earth an hour after take-off.

If space travel is too costly at the speeds needed to reduce ageing to this extent, there is a cheaper alternative. And if it will not work for everything, it will at least work for people and other organisms, which are what really concern us. This technique uses the fact, exploited in refrigerators, that most organic processes, like other chemical reactions, go slower at lower temperatures. That fact enables us in principle, if not yet safely in practice, to travel into the future by freezing ourselves for the duration and then thawing out again. Hibernation also slows down bodily processes to some extent, and to that extent is a way of travelling forward in time – indeed the only way so far devised that is both safe and practical. In short, every hibernating animal is a time traveller, and so was Rip van Winkle.

All in all, what is called forward time travel is neither a problematic nor an especially remarkable phenomenon. To call it that is simply to give a misleadingly portentous description of situations in which our mental and bodily processes take longer than they normally do.

12 *The linearity of time*

1 Backward time travel

If forward time travel is just a misnomer for unusually slow processes, backward time travel is another matter altogether. It threatens not just the metric but the linear topology of time that I have so far taken for granted. Several other topologies have been tacitly dismissed already, notably the 'branching' times in which alternative actual futures diverge from a single present and past. These of course make no sense on the B-theory of time I have argued for. What remains to be seen is whether our causal B-theory can allow timelike loops, either the local loops that backward time travel needs, or the universal loop of circular time. Let us start with the former.

It is not immediately obvious that our B-theory rules out backward time travel. After all, if we can travel forward in time by slowing down our processes, why not backward by reversing them? Since many natural processes are indeed reversible, might we not be able, at least in principle, to reverse those of perception, memory, action and physiological decay?

The reply to this rhetorical question has two parts. The first part starts by noting that some processes, like electrons repelling each other, are made irreversible by laws of nature, and these we cannot reverse. That however does not stop us reversing processes of a less specific type, namely of two particles moving apart, by replacing one electron with a positron. This, as we saw in chapter 11.1, is like reversing the clockwise motion of a clock by replacing its clockwork with that of an anti-clockwise clock. Why then, if we can do this, can we not reverse the mental and bodily processes that distress us as we age by a suitable replacement of their 'clockwork'?

Perhaps we can: perhaps there is an elixir of youth which, if only we could find it, would rejuvenate us. But nice though that might be, it would not, for the reasons given in chapter 11.1, make us any more capable than positrons or anti-clockwise clocks are of travelling back in time. Reversing our ageing processes is, however attractive, as irrelevant to backward time travel as reversing any other process is. For no elixir of youth will reverse the mechanisms of perception, memory and action in the only sense that matters here, which is the causal one. By this I mean that it will not let us

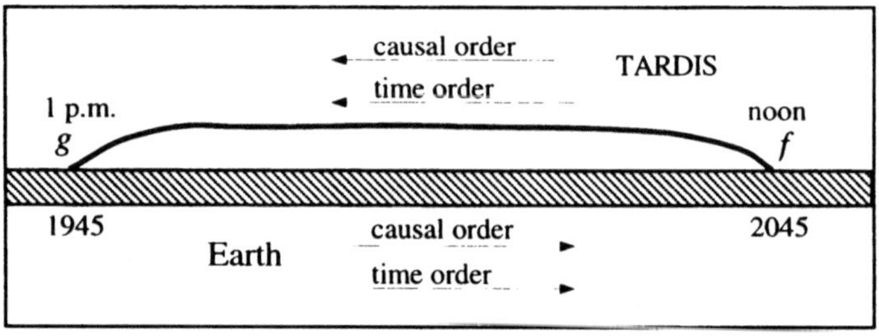

Figure 11

affect our past or recall our future, as for example Dr Who could do if his time machine TARDIS really could go back in time.

For suppose that Dr Who did travel back from 2045 to 1945, leaving (f) at noon and arriving (g) an hour later by TARDIS time, as shown above in Figure 11. His actions before he leaves, e.g. his choice of clothes, would affect what for him are the later events of 1945 (e.g. by causing a fashion for his futuristic scarves). This is one way in which his trip would make our future affect our past. Another is his ability to recall in the London of 1945 what he saw and did an hour earlier in 2045. In these and many other ways Dr Who's backward time travel tale, like all such tales, relies on backward causation, just as our causal theory of time order requires.

This backward causation need not of course be unmediated. All the 1945 effects of 2045 causes that his trip produces can be mediated by causation working in TARDIS just as it does outside. All Dr Who's mental and bodily processes, all his computers and other machinery, will work there as they do elsewhere. Indeed nothing about the causation within TARDIS need show it to be a time machine at all. What does that is its arriving a century before it departs, thereby forming the closed causal and timelike loop of Figure 11. Loops like this are all we need in order to travel back in time. Can we have them?

One objection to the loop in Figure 11 we may dismiss at once. This is that it gives f and g, the events that close the loop by linking TARDIS to the outside world, two incompatible time relations, by making f both a century later and an hour earlier than g. But there need be no inconsistency in this, or at least not in the difference between an hour and a century. Different paths between the same two points in spacetime can easily have different lengths, as we saw in §4. The problem here, if there is one, lies not in the different lengths of the two paths linking f and g but in the opposite time order they give those events, by making f earlier than g in TARDIS and later than g in the world outside. But the impossibility even of this is not obvious enough to be taken for granted. To show that there can be no causal and hence timelike loops needs an argument which has not yet been given.

On the other hand, it is no more obvious that such loops are possible than that they are not. Their possibility also needs arguing for, and at least four well-known arguments for it will not do. One, made famous by Gödel (1949), infers the possibility of timelike loops from their consistency with the equations of general relativity. But this consistency proves nothing: all it shows is that general relativity does not rule them out, not that nothing does. (Gödel's argument illustrates the common and pernicious fallacy that nothing can show what physics cannot show, so that anything which is physically possible, i.e. consistent with physics, must be possible in fact.)

The other three arguments for the possibility of backward time travel are all replies to the most familiar if elusive objection to it. This is that Dr Who could on arriving in 1945 do something (like killing his grandmother in her infancy) which would cause him never to leave in 2045 (by causing him never to exist), thus generating a contradiction in his time travel tale.

The first reply to this, common in time travel fiction, is to tell the tale twice over, first 'before' the travel and then 'after' it. Thus time-travelling dinosaur hunters try to minimise the risk to their own future existence by only shooting animals which a previous reconnaissance has shown to be dying an instant later anyway. But this reply of course just makes matters worse, for by saying that a dinosaur both is and is not shot it replaces a merely possible contradiction with an actual one.

The second reply tries to avoid contradiction by placing the dinosaur's shooting, or Dr Who's arrival in 1945, in another possible world. But this will not do either, because it sets up a fatal trilemma. First, it may mean that the time travel turns the actual world from one where it has not occurred into one where it has. But this is the same contradiction, since the actual world cannot both contain and not contain Dr Who in 1945. But then, second, *no* possible world can contain such a contradictory state of affairs. Nothing that is logically impossible in our world can occur in any other possible world, since saying that it does is just a way of saying that it *is* possible in our world. So, third, the world where Dr Who arrives in 1945 must differ from the world where he sets off in 2045. But this too is simply a way of saying that backward time travel cannot occur within any one possible world, and so in particular cannot occur in ours.

The third and best reply just requires time travel tales to be consistent, as all tales must be if they are to be capable of truth (Lewis 1976). So of course, if Dr Who does leave in 2045, he can do nothing in 1945 that would stop himself leaving. This is a trivial consistency condition, and easily satisfied, since Dr Who does not *have* to do anything that would stop him leaving later. There are many ways in which he and the rest of us can act after his arrival in 1945 that will *not* make his time travel tale inconsistent. If that is so, as it clearly is, then his tale can be true, i.e. the situation shown in Figure 11 is possible.

What is wrong with this reply? The short answer is that it overlooks the existence of real contingent possibilities. Dr Who may not *need* to do anything in 1945 that would in fact stop him setting out in 2045, but he *could*. This seems to me as obvious a fact about him at that time as any fact about what he actually does then. So Figure 11 must be consistent with it. But it is not, as we have just seen, since it is *necessarily* impossible for Dr Who to do anything that would make his time travel tale inconsistent; and nothing can be contingently possible that is necessarily impossible. So his backward time travel tale, like all such tales, must be false.

2 The chances of causation

This short answer, although right, cannot be the last word, for two reasons. First, it assumes that there are contingent facts about what is possible at a time, as well as about what is actual, and that is contentious. Second, it does not tell us what these contingent possibilities have to do with causation, and so with backward causation and time travel. What does tell us this is a part of the theory of *The Facts of Causation* (*FoC*) that I have not yet invoked. There I argue, on quite different grounds, that (i) all effects need chances, with and without their causes, which (ii) are contingent possibilities of the very kind we need. The argument for (i) is in chapters 2, 6 and 7 of *FoC*, and for (ii) in chapters 3 and 4; here I just summarise the results I require.

First, a factual cause C is *sufficient for* an effect E (in the circumstances – a proviso I shall hereafter take as read) if and only if it makes E's chance of existing 1, i.e. makes it impossible, in the contingent sense that concerns us, for E not to exist. Thus, in the example of chapter 9.3, *a*'s cooling is sufficient for *b*'s freezing if and only if it gives *b* a zero chance of *not* freezing. Second, C is *necessary for* E if and only if E cannot, in this contingent sense, exist without C, i.e. if ~C gives E a zero chance of existing. Thus *a*'s cooling is necessary for *b*'s freezing if and only if *b* has a zero chance of freezing if *a* does not cool.

If C is both sufficient and necessary for E, I call it a *deterministic* cause of E. But causation need not be deterministic, since causes need be neither sufficient nor necessary for their effects. Smoking, for example, can cause me to get cancer even if my chance of getting it is less than 1 if I do smoke, and greater than 0 if I do not. But what then does C's causing E require of E's chance? I argue in *FoC* that it requires C to raise E's chance, since otherwise C would not be evidence for E, or explain it, or be a means to it – all of which I argue follow from C's causing E. This is why no one will say, if I get cancer without ever smoking, that my cancer's causes include my *not* smoking. For since this fact lowers my chance of getting cancer, it is not evidence that I will get it, will not explain my getting it if I do, and would not be a means to that perverse end.

The case for taking all causes to raise the chances of their effects seems to me overwhelming. Yet as some still deny this thesis, and I do not need it here, I shall not assume it. All I need here is its less contentious consequence that, in the relevant circumstances, every effect *has* chances with and without its causes. I have chances of getting cancer if I smoke and if I do not; *b* has chances of freezing if *a* cools and if it does not; and so on.

What are these chances? I say they are possibilities of a kind that is not only contingent but comes by degrees, ranging from zero (impossible) to 1 (necessary). If P is a possible or even impossible fact (i.e. a state of affairs in the sense of chapter 2.2), then a chance of P, which I write *ch*(P), is a possibility that P is an actual fact. The corresponding chance that P is *not* an actual fact, so that ~P is, is 1–*ch*(P). Thus if a coin toss has a 3/4 chance of landing heads, it also has a 1/4 chance of not doing so.

Chances are therefore quantitative properties, like temperatures. Only unlike temperatures they are not properties of the facts that we apparently ascribe them to. For while a thing *a* can only have one temperature at a time, a fact P can have many different chances. A coin's chance of landing heads may vary from 3/4 as it is tossed to 1/10 as it is about to land, with many other chances in between. And this is not like *a*'s having different temperatures at different times, since *a* can only have its temperatures when and where *a* itself is. But all a coin toss's chances of landing heads are located *earlier* than the fact that it lands heads – even if that fact exists, which of course it will not do if the toss actually lands tails.

A fact P's chances can therefore not be properties of that fact, any more than, as we saw in chapter 8.3, your fame can be a property of you, and for the same reason: P's chances lie elsewhere and can exist even if P does not, just as non-existent people like Hamlet can be famous. This is why *ch*(P) can be both high (as a coin is tossed) and low (as it falls tails up), just as you can be both famous (in Australia) and unknown (in Italy). In neither case is this a contradiction, as the incompatible properties are properties of different entities, in your case of Australians and Italians, in P's case of – what? Of what, if not of P, are P's chances properties?

The answer is that they are properties of facts earlier than P (or earlier than ~P, if that is the fact). If P is our coin toss's landing heads, P's 3/4 chance is a property of how the coin is tossed, P's 1/10 chance a property of how it is falling before it lands, and so on. And as these chances are properties of those facts, so they are located when and where those facts are. Our coin's 3/4 chance of landing heads is located when and where it is tossed, its 1/10 chance when and where it falls, and so on.

And as for chances generally, so for the chances of effects. An effect E has many chances, each of which is a property of some fact earlier than E. What then do I mean by *the* chance which a cause C gives E? I mean the *ch*(E) which is a property of a conjunctive fact that includes C and all the other facts (mostly coincident with C in space and time) which constitute the relevant circumstances. Thus suppose for example that a short circuit in a mixture of oxygen and fuel causes an explosion. Let these facts – that there is a short circuit, oxygen, fuel and an explosion – be C, O, F and E respectively. Then the chance that C gives E is the *ch*(E), say p, that is a property of the fact O&F&C. Similarly, E's chance *without* C is the *ch*(E), say p', that *would* be a property of O&F&~C if, in the circumstances O&F, ~C was the fact, i.e. if there was no short circuit.

It is then a fact about the circumstances O&F that in them *ch*(E) is p if C is a fact and p' if ~C is. It is a fact about an oxygen/fuel mixture that in it the chance of an explosion is p with a short circuit and p' without. In this case of course p is high and p' is low (if the causation is deterministic p will be 1 and p' 0). But this fact, like the fact that p exceeds p', which I say is necessary for a short circuit to cause an explosion, is contingent, since it is contingent on the contingent laws of combustion. The fact that laws fix the values of p and p' does not stop p and p' being logically independent.

And as in this case, so I say in all others. In order to have any effect E any cause C needs a conjunction of two logically independent facts, about what in the relevant circumstances E's chances p and p', with and without C, are. But what then are these facts: what are their constituents?

The answer, once seen, is obvious: they are particulars with properties like mass. Any net force F will always cause any thing a with any mass M to accelerate at F/M: why? Because M is the property of a that makes the chances p and p', of a's accelerating at F/M with and without any net force F, 1 and 0 respectively. (The fact that in this case a single truthmaker Ma entails both p and p' does not stop them being logically independent. Again it is contingent laws of nature, in this case of classical mechanics, that make the property of mass exist and fix the chances of things accelerating as they do under different forces.)

Similarly for other deterministic properties like momentum, energy, pressure, temperature, charge, etc., as readers can easily verify. Similarly too for indeterministic properties, like the biases of coins, the half-lives of radioactive atoms and the metabolic properties that give us our chances of getting cancer if we smoke and if we do not.

The fact is that all causation, deterministic and indeterministic, needs particulars with such properties, properties that I therefore call *causal*. It is the causal properties of particulars that give effects the chances they need, with and without their causes, in order to *be* effects of those causes. And it is the logical independence of the chances that causal properties entail which, as we shall see in §4, makes time linear by ruling out the causal and hence the timelike loops that cyclical time and backward time travel need.

3 The logical independence of causal facts

Suppose that my friend Jim's racing on 2 June causes him to have a fatal heart attack, that this causal fact is itself caused by his having a weak heart, and that it in turn causes the racing to be stopped. That is,

(i) Jim dies because he races, because he has a weak heart, and
(ii) the racing is stopped, because Jim dies because he races.

This shows how the fact that C causes E may itself have causes and effects, and these may or may not also be causes or effects of C or E. Thus I take it in (ii) that the racing is also stopped because Jim dies, whereas in (i) Jim does not race because he has a weak heart. It could however be the other way round. In (ii) the racing might not be stopped just because Jim dies, but only because he dies because he races. Conversely, in (i) Jim could also have raced because he had a weak heart, because he wanted to prove that his new-found fitness made it safe for him to do so.

In general therefore the fact that C causes E may, although it need not, depend causally on other facts, including causes of C. But not logically. If Jim's having a weak heart causes him to race, or to die because he races, these facts, like all other such facts, are contingent. Neither of them makes the fact that Jim dies because he races depend logically on his having a weak heart. That causal fact is as logically independent of the causes of his racing as it is of the effects of his dying.

In short, just as the contingency of causation stops C and E entailing that C causes E, so it stops the fact that C causes E entailing anything about its own causes or effects, or about any causes of C or effects of E. This is why all parties, whether they take causation to relate facts or events, take it to be a two-term relation. By this I mean that if C causes E, this fact is logically independent of specific facts other than those entailed by C and E, which it entails. (If C and E are not contiguous, the fact that C causes E may entail that there are intermediate causes and effects, but it does not entail what they are.) It is not, for example, like distant simultaneity, an apparently two-term relation which, as we saw in chapter 1.4, special relativity says has a third term, namely a reference frame.

If then, as argued in §2, the causation that links C and E is embodied in conjunctive facts about E's chances with and without C, such conjunctions must be as logically independent of each other as we saw in §2 that their conjuncts are. And so they are. The fact that a thing *a* has a changeable property *F* at a time *t′* may, as we saw in chapter 9.4, depend causally on *a*'s having been *F* at an earlier time *t*. But not logically, since, as calling *F* changeable implies, there is no contradiction in *a*'s being *F* at *t* but not at *t′*.

And all causal properties of things are always changeable. Even when conservation laws stop the masses, momenta or energies of things changing, there is no more contradiction in taking these causal properties to change than there is in taking light to travel faster than relativity allows. Here, as in the examples of §2, it is only the laws of nature, not of consistency, that constrain changes in these properties. There is likewise no contradiction in taking the causal properties of particulars to vary – or not to vary – across space, as for example the temperatures of things and events, the intensities of fields, and the curvature of spacetime may do.

From this it follows in particular that for no cause C and effect E do E's logically independent chances with and without C entail anything about the equally independent chances of C with and without its causes, or about the chances of E's effects with and without E. For on our causal theory of time order, if C's *B*-time is *t*, E's must be a later *B*-time *t′*. So while E's chances with and without C depend on the causal properties of particulars at *t*, C's chances with and without its causes depend on those of particulars at earlier times; just as the chances of E's effects depend on those at the later time *t′*. And then the logical independence of the causal properties that particulars have at different times will stop any of these chances entailing each other.

4 The impossibility of causal loops

Now consider an *n*-sided causal loop, like loop A in Figure 12 opposite. In A a fact P_1 causes a fact P_2, which causes a fact P_3, and so on … until the loop is closed by a fact P_n causing P_1. Can there be such a loop?

Before answering this question I shall first use the logical independence of the causal facts in A to simplify it. For if all these facts are independent, then the fact that P_1 causes P_2 must be independent of the causes of P_1 and the effects of P_2. But then if A is possible, so is any loop derived from it by making internally consistent assumptions about P_1's causes and P_2's effects. In particular then we may assume that P_2 itself, by causing P_3, which causes P_4, and so on … eventually, via P_{n-1} and P_n, causes P_1. For while, as I noted in chapter 11.1, causation may not be transitive, it is certainly not

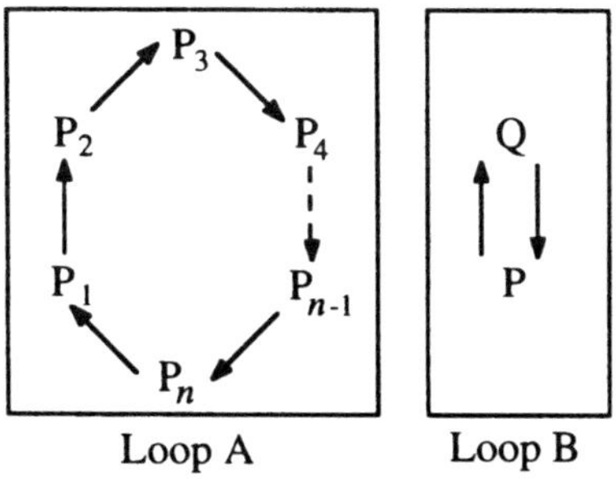

Figure 12

*in*transitive. That is, even if C's causing D and D's causing E do not entail that C causes E, they certainly do not entail that C does *not* cause E.

So even if, in loop A, P_2 does not cause P_4 by causing P_3, cause P_5 by causing P_4, and so on, all the way round to P_1, there is no inconsistency in supposing that it does. Hence Figure 12's loop B, where P is P_1 and Q is P_2. If A is possible, so is B. Conversely, if B is impossible, i.e. if no fact P can both cause and be caused by another fact Q, then A and all other causal loops will also be impossible. And B *is* impossible, as we shall now see.

On the theory of causation outlined in §2, Q can only cause P if it is a property of Q's circumstances that P has a chance p with Q, and a logically independent chance p' without Q. Similarly, P can only cause Q if it is a property of P's circumstances that Q has a chance q with P and a logically independent chance q' without P. And as it follows from the causal theory of time order that P and Q have different locations in spacetime, so it also follows, for the reasons given in §3, that p and p' are logically independent of q and q'. So if B is possible, all combinations of individually possible values of p, p', q and q' must also be possible. But they are not.

To show why not, I must first say how chances are related to relevant fractions (often called 'relative frequencies') by the so-called *laws of large numbers*. Take for example a sequence of n actual or hypothetical coin tosses on each of which the chance of heads is q. As n increases, so does the chance that the relative frequency (i.e. fraction) f_n of these tosses which land heads will be close to q. Specifically, as n increases without limit, f_n's chance of differing from q by less than any given amount, however small, while it will never be 1, will eventually differ from 1 by less than any given amount, however small.

From this law of large numbers it follows in particular that the greater the chance p of heads on one toss, the higher is the fraction of heads in many such tosses almost certain to be. And that of course is what we should expect if chances are contingent possibilities. Tosses that cannot land heads will never land heads. Tosses that must land heads will always land heads. And in between, the greater the possibility of heads on any one toss, the more often we should expect such tosses to land heads.

Similarly for chances of effects with and without their causes. Suppose a man a's chances of getting cancer are q if he smokes and q' if he does not, and suppose many (n) people share these chances. Among these n people, let the fractions of smokers and of non-smokers who get cancer be f_n and f'_n. Then if q is greater than q', the chance of f_n being greater than f'_n will be far higher than the chance of f_n being less than f'_n. In words: if smoking raises many people's chances of getting cancer, the chance that a greater fraction of smokers than of non-smokers will get cancer is far higher than the chance that a lesser fraction will. And similarly in all other cases, including the four chances p, p', q and q' in loop B.

Suppose then that, in B, P is a's smoking and Q is a's getting cancer. Next, imagine 20 million (20m) people with a's chances q and q' of getting cancer if they do and do not smoke. Of these, let the numbers of smokers and non-smokers, N(P) and N(~P), both be 10m, and suppose q=0.6 and q'=0.2. Then it is almost certain that very close to 6m of our 10m smokers, and 2m of our 10m non-smokers, will get cancer. So of our 20m people, the numbers with and without cancer are almost certain to be very close to 8m and 12m respectively, facts I shall write 'N(Q)≈8m' and 'N(~Q)≈12m'.

This is how the laws of large numbers make the number of people like a who get cancer depend on (i) their chances p and p' of getting cancer if they do and do not smoke, and (ii) how many of them smoke and how many do not, i.e. on N(P) and N(~P). And if, as in B, P not only causes but is caused by Q, the laws of large numbers will also apply the other way. The number of people like a who smoke will depend on (i) their chances p and p' of smoking if they do and do not get cancer, and (ii) how many get cancer, N(Q), and how many do not, N(~Q).

But we know already that N(Q) and N(~Q) are almost certainly close to 8m and 12m. We also know that p and p' are logically independent of q and q'. So provided p is not 0 (since P is a fact) p and p' can take any value between 0 and 1. So suppose p is 0.5 and p' is 0.25. Then it is almost certain that very nearly 4m of the approximately 8m people like a who get cancer, and 3m of the approximately 12m of them who do not get cancer, will smoke. So of our 20m people, the number who smoke is almost certain to be very close to 7m, so that N(P)≈7m and N(~P)≈13m. All this is shown in Figure 13.

But this, as Figure 13 shows, contradicts our initial hypothesis of equal numbers of smokers and non-smokers like a. The fact that N(P) is 10m and

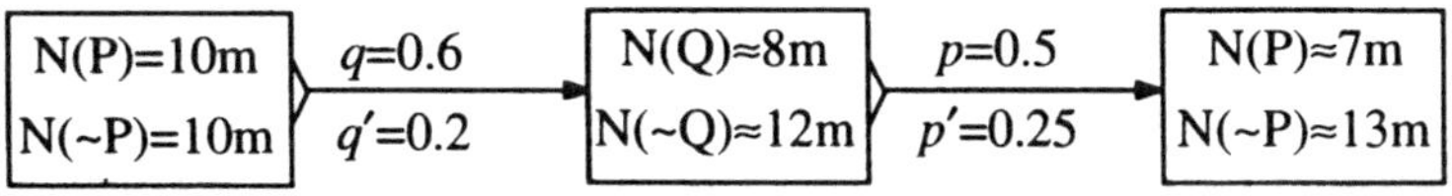

Figure 13

N(~P) is 10m cannot possibly make it almost certain that N(P) is around 7m and N(~P) is around 13m! Yet this is what loop B will entail if p, p', q and q' are 0.5, 0.25, 0.6 and 0.2; and many other values of these four chances will make B entail similar contradictions.

Yet since, as we saw in §§2–3, p, p', q and q' are logically independent of each other, all combinations of them must be logically possible if B is. But some are impossible; so B is impossible. If Q has logically independent chances with and without P, P cannot also have such chances with and without Q. This is why Q cannot cause P if P causes Q: the constraints that P's causing Q puts on Q's possibilities prevent Q's causing P, and hence putting independent constraints on P's possibilities. And this fact in turn, on a causal theory of time order, and the chancy theory of causation outlined in §2, explains why no fact P has any chances, zero or otherwise, that are properties of facts later than P.

But if Figure 12's loop B is impossible so, as we saw in §3, is its loop A. So there can be no such causal loops, however long. In particular, then, Figure 11 is impossible: Dr Who cannot travel back from 2045 to 1945, since the backward causation that his trip needs cannot, as it would have to, limit the independent possibilities of his actions in the nineteen-forties.

In short, the classic objection to backward time travel given in §1 is right after all. If Dr Who's trip were possible, he could make it impossible by killing his grandmother in her infancy. But since what is logically possible cannot also be possibly impossible, if his trip was logically possible he could not possibly kill his grandmother then. So as he obviously could kill his grandmother then, his trip is impossible. Wherever Dr Who's time machine comes from when it lands in the present, it cannot be the future.

And as for backward time travel so, finally, for cyclical time, since the case against causal loops in no way depends on there being anything outside them: loop A in Figure 12 could include the whole history of the world. This then is how our causal theory of time order rules out cyclical time, by making cyclical time entail that our present and future actions could affect our past. But that, as we have seen, they could not do. So time cannot go round in a circle. Therefore since, on a *B*-theory of time, it can also not branch, it must be linear; as of course it is.

Bibliography

Works referred to are listed below together with other relevant and recent (mostly post-1981) works in English. (Articles in listed collections are not listed separately.) Where two dates are given, the first is the date of first publication, the second that of the publication cited.

Adams, R. M. (1986) 'Time and Thisness', *Midwest Studies in Philosophy* **11**, 315–29.

Armstrong, D. M. (1997) *A World of States of Affairs*, Cambridge: Cambridge University Press.

Arntzenius, F. (1995) 'Indeterminism and the Direction of Time', *Topoi* **14**, 67–81.

Augustynek, Z. et al. (1991) *Time: Past, Present, Future*, Dordrecht: Kluwer.

Baxter, D. L. M. (1989) 'Identity through Time and the Discernibility of Identicals', *Analysis* **49**, 125–31.

Beer, M. (1988) 'Temporal Indexicals and the Passage of Time', *Philosophical Quarterly* **38**, 158–64.

Belnap Jr, N. D. (1992) 'Branching Space-Time', *Synthese* **92**, 385–434.

Bennett, J. (1984) 'Counterfactuals and Temporal Direction', *Philosophical Review* **93**, 57–97.

Bernstein, M. (1990) 'Fatalism Revisited', *Metaphilosophy* **21**, 270–81.

Bigelow, J. (1991) 'Worlds Enough for Time', *Noûs* **25**, 1–19.

Brown, B. (1992) 'Defending Backwards Causation', *Canadian Journal of Philosophy* **22**, 429–43.

Buller, D. J. and Foster, T. R. (1992) 'The New Paradox of Temporal Transience', *Philosophical Quarterly* **42**, 357–66.

Butterfield, J. (1984) 'Seeing the Present', *Mind* **93**, 161–76.

(1985a) 'Indexicals and Tense', *Exercises in Analysis*, ed. I. Hacking, Cambridge: Cambridge University Press, 69–87.

(1985b) 'Spatial and Temporal Parts', *Philosophical Quarterly* **35**, 32–44.

Carter, W. S. and Hestevold, H. S. (1994) 'On Passage and Persistence', *American Philosophical Quarterly* **31**, 269–83.

Chapman, T. (1982) *Time: A Philosophical Analysis*, Dordrecht: Reidel.

Chisholm, R. M. (1990) 'Events Without Times: An Essay on Ontology', *Noûs* **24**, 413–27.

Christensen, F. M. (1987) 'Time's Error: Is Time's Asymmetry Extrinsic?', *Erkenntnis* **26**, 231–48.

(1993) *Space-Like Time*, Toronto: University of Toronto Press.

Cleland, C. E. (1990) 'The Difference Between Real Change and *Mere* Cambridge Change', *Philosophical Studies* **60**, 257–80.

Clifton, R. and Hogarth, M. (1995) 'The Definability of Objective Becoming in Minkowski Spacetime', *Synthese* **103**, 355–87.

Cockburn, D. (1987) 'The Problem of the Past', *Philosophical Quarterly* **37**, 54–77.

Craig, W. L. (1988) 'Tachyons, Time Travel and Divine Omniscience', *Journal of Philosophy* **85**, 135–50.

(1996a) 'The New B-Theory's "Tu Quoque" Argument', *Synthese* **107**, 249–69.

(1996b) 'Tense and the New B-Theory of Language', *Philosophy* **71**, 5–26.

Cresswell, M. J. (1990) 'Modality and Mellor's McTaggart', *Studia Logica* **49**, 163–70.

Davidson, D. (1967) 'Causal Relations', *Causation*, ed. E. Sosa and M. Tooley (1993), Oxford: Oxford University Press, 75–87.

(1980) *Essays on Actions and Events*, Oxford: Clarendon Press.

Dennett, D. C. (1991) *Consciousness Explained*, London: Penguin.

Deutsch, H. (1990) 'Real Possibility', *Noûs* **24**, 751–5.

Dieks, D. (1988) 'Special Relativity and the Flow of Time', *Philosophy of Science* **55**, 456–60.

Dorato, M. (1995) *Time and Reality: Spacetime Physics and the Objectivity of Temporal Becoming*, Bologna: Cooperativa Libraria Universitaria Editrice Bologna (CLUEB).

Dowden, B. H. (1991) 'A Linear Continuum of Time', *Philosophia Mathematica* **6**, 53–64.

Dowe, P. (1992) 'Process Causality and Asymmetry', *Erkenntnis* **37**, 179–96.

Dummett, M. (1964) 'Bringing About the Past', *Truth and Other Enigmas* (1978), London: Duckworth, 333–50.

Earman, J. (1989) *World Enough and Space-Time*, Cambridge, Mass.: MIT Press.

(1993) ed., *Philosophical Problems of the Internal and External Worlds*, Pittsburgh: University of Pittsburgh Press.

(1995) 'Outlawing Time Machines: Chronology Protection Theorems', *Erkenntnis* **42**, 125–39.

Edwards, A. M. (1995) 'Springing Forward and Falling Back: Travelling through Time', *Contemporary Philosophy* **17**, 12–24.

Ehring, D. (1987) 'Personal Identity and Time Travel', *Philosophical Studies* **52**, 427–33.

Elias, N. (1992) *Time: an Essay*, Oxford: Blackwell.

Farmer, D. J. (1990) *Being in Time: The Nature of Time in Light of McTaggart's Paradox*, Lanham: University Press of America.

Faye, J. (1989) *The Reality of the Future*, Odense: Odense University Press.

(1993) 'Is the Future Really Real?', *American Philosophical Quarterly* **30**, 259–69.

Faye, J. et al., eds (1997) *Perspectives on Time*, Dordrecht: Kluwer.

Feinberg, G. (1992) 'Knowledge of the Past and Future', *Journal of Philosophy* **89**, 607–42.

Felt, J. W. (1992) 'Fatalism and Truth about the Future', *Thomist* **56**, 209–27.

Fitch, G. W. (1994) 'Singular Propositions in Time', *Philosophical Studies* **73**, 181–7.

Flew, A. (1988) 'Time Travel and the Paranormal', *Philosophy* **63**, 266–8.

Flood, R. and Lockwood, M., eds (1986) *The Nature of Time*, Oxford: Blackwell.

Freddoso, A. J. (1982) 'Accidental Necessity and Power over the Past', *Pacific Philosophical Quarterly* **63**, 54–68.

Friedman, M. (1983) *Foundations of Space-Time Theories*, Princeton: Princeton University Press.

Gallois, A. (1994) 'Asymmetry in Attitudes and the Nature of Time', *Philosophical Studies* **76**, 51–69.

Garrett, B. (1988) '"Thank Goodness That's Over" Revisited', *Philosophical Quarterly* **38**, 201–5.

Gödel, K. (1949) 'A Remark about the Relationship between Relativity Theory and Idealistic Philosophy', *Albert Einstein: Philosopher–Scientist*, ed. P. A. Schilpp, La Salle, Illinois: Open Court, 557–62.

Goodman, N. (1965) *Fact, Fiction, and Forecast*, 2nd edn, New York: Bobbs-Merrill.

Hacker, P. M. S. (1982) 'Events and Objects in Space and Time', *Mind* **92**, 1–19.

Hardin, C. L. (1984) '"Thank Goodness It's Over There"', *Philosophy* **59**, 121–5.

Harris, E. E. (1988) *The Reality Of Time*, Albany: SUNY Press.

Hawking, S. W. (1988) *A Brief History of Time*, London: Bantam Books.

Hawking, S. W. and Ellis, G. F. R. (1973) *The Large-Scale Structure of Space-Time*, Cambridge: Cambridge University Press.

Healey, R. A., ed. (1981) *Reduction, Time and Reality*, Cambridge: Cambridge University Press.

(1992) 'Causation, Robustness, and EPR', *Philosophy of Science* **59**, 282–92.

Heller, M. (1991) *The Ontology of Physical Objects*, Cambridge: Cambridge University Press.

(1992) 'Things Change', *Philosophy and Phenomenological Research* **52**, 695–704.

Hestevold, H. S. (1990) 'Passage and the Presence of Experience', *Philosophy and Phenomenological Research* **50**, 537–52.

Higginbotham, J. (1995) 'Tensed Thoughts', *Mind and Language* **10**, 226–49.

Horwich, P. (1987) *Asymmetries in Time*, Cambridge, Mass.: MIT Press.

Jeffrey, R. C. (1980) 'Coming True', *Intention and Intentionality*, ed. C. Diamond and J. Teichman, London: Harvester, 251–60.

Kant, I. (1781) *Critique of Pure Reason*, English edn, transl. N. Kemp Smith, (1933), London: Macmillan.

Kaplan, D. (1989) 'Demonstratives', *Themes from Kaplan*, ed. J. Almog et al., Oxford: Oxford University Press, 481–563.

Kim, J. (1976) 'Events as Property Exemplifications', *Action Theory*, ed. M. Brand and D. Walton, Dordrecht: Reidel, 159–77.

Kline, G. L. (1986) '"Present", "Past" and "Future" as Categoreal Terms, and the "Fallacy of the Actual Future"', *Review of Metaphysics* **40**, 215–35.

Kroes, P. (1984) 'Objective versus Mind-Dependent Theories of Time Flow', *Synthese* **61**, 423–47.

Landsberg, P. T., ed. (1982) *The Enigma of Time*, Bristol: Hilger.

Le Poidevin, R. (1988) 'Time and Truth in Fiction', *British Journal of Aesthetics* **28**, 248–58.

(1991) *Change, Cause and Contradiction*, London: Macmillan.

(1992) 'On the Acausality of Time, Space, and Space-Time', *Analysis* **52**, 146–54.

(1996) 'Time, Tense and Topology', *Philosophical Quarterly* **46**, 467–81.

Le Poidevin, R. and MacBeath, M., eds (1993) *The Philosophy of Time*, Oxford: Oxford University Press.

Le Poidevin, R. and Mellor, D. H. (1987) 'Time, Change and the "Indexical Fallacy"', *Mind* **96**, 534–8.

Leibniz, G. W. and Clarke, S. (1717) *The Leibniz–Clarke Correspondence*, ed. H. G. Alexander, (1956), Manchester: Manchester University Press.

Levison, A. B. (1987) 'Events and Time's Flow', *Mind* **76**, 341–53.

Lewis, D. (1976) 'The Paradoxes of Time Travel', *Philosophical Papers Volume II* (1986), Oxford: Oxford University Press, 67–80.

Lewis, D. (1979a) 'Attitudes *De Dicto* and *De Se* [plus Postscripts]', *Philosophical Papers Volume I* (1983), Oxford: Oxford University Press, 133–59.
(1979b) 'Counterfactual Dependence and Time's Arrow', *Philosophical Papers Volume II* (1986), Oxford: Oxford University Press, 32–52.
Lieb, I. C. (1992) *Past, Present and Future: A Philosophical Essay about Time*, Champaign: University of Illinois Press.
Loizou, A. (1986) *The Reality of Time*, Brookfield: Gower.
Lowe, E. J. (1987) 'The Indexical Fallacy in McTaggart's Proof of the Unreality of Time', *Mind* **96**, 62–70.
Lucas, J. R. (1984) *Space, Time and Causality*, Oxford: Clarendon Press.
(1989) *The Future: An Essay on God, Temporality, and Truth*, Oxford: Blackwell.
MacBeath, M. (1982) 'Who was Dr Who's Father?', *Synthese* **51**, 397–430.
(1983) 'Mellor's Emeritus Headache', *Ratio* **25**, 81–8.
(1986) 'Clipping Time's Wings', *Mind* **95**, 233–7.
Markosian, N. (1992) 'On Language and the Passage of Time', *Philosophical Studies* **66**, 1–26.
(1993) 'How Fast does Time Pass?', *Philosophy and Phenomenological Research* **53**, 829–44.
Maudlin, T. (1990) 'Time-Travel and Topology', *Proceedings of the Biennial Meetings of the Philosophy of Science Association*, 303–15.
(1994) *Quantum Non-Locality and Relativity*, Oxford: Blackwell.
McCall, S. (1984) 'A Dynamic Model of Temporal Becoming', *Analysis* **44**, 172–6.
(1994) *A Model of the Universe: Spacetime, Probability and Decision*, Oxford: Clarendon Press.
McInerney, P. K. (1991) *Time and Experience*, Philadelphia: Temple University Press.
McTaggart, J. M. E. (1908) 'The Unreality of Time', *Mind* **18**, 457–84.
(1927) *The Nature of Existence*, Cambridge: Cambridge University Press.
Mellor, D. H. (1980) 'On Things and Causes in Spacetime', *British Journal for the Philosophy of Science* **31**, 282–8.
(1981) 'McTaggart, Fixity and Coming True', *Matters of Metaphysics* (1991), Cambridge: Cambridge University Press, 183–200.
(1983) 'MacBeath's Soluble Aspirin', *Ratio* **25**, 89–92.
(1989) 'I and Now', *Matters of Metaphysics* (1991), Cambridge: Cambridge University Press, 17–29.
(1991) 'Properties and Predicates', *Properties*, ed. D. H. Mellor and A. Oliver (1997), Oxford: Oxford University Press, 254–67.
(1995) *The Facts of Causation*, London: Routledge.
Merricks, T. (1995) 'On the Incompatibility of Enduring and Perduring Entities', *Mind* **104**, 523–31.
Myro, G. (1986) 'Time and Essence', *Midwest Studies in Philosophy* **11**, 331–41.
Nerlich, G. (1994) *What Spacetime Explains*, Cambridge: Cambridge University Press.
Newton, I. (1713) *Mathematical Principles of Natural Philosophy*, transl. A. Motte, ed. F. Cajori, (1962), Berkeley: University of California Press.
Newton-Smith, W. H. (1980) *The Structure of Time*, London: Routledge & Kegan Paul.
Ni, P. (1992) 'Changing the Past', *Noûs* **26**, 349–59.
Noonan, H. W. (1985) 'A Note on Temporal Parts', *Analysis* **45**, 151–2.
Oaklander, L. N. (1984) *Temporal Relations and Temporal Becoming*, Lanham: University Press of America.

Oaklander, L. N. (1991) 'A Defence of the New Tenseless Theory of Time', *Philosophical Quarterly* **41**, 26–38.
(1992) 'Temporal Passage and Temporal Parts', *Noûs* **26**, 79–84.
(1993) 'On the Experience of Tenseless Time', *Journal of Philosophical Research* **18**, 159–66.
(1994) 'Bigelow, Possible Worlds and the Passage of Time', *Analysis* **54**, 244–8.
(1996) 'McTaggart's Paradox and Smith's Tensed Theory of Time', *Synthese* **107**, 205–21.
Oaklander, L. N. and Smith, Q., eds (1994) *The New Theory of Time*, New Haven: Yale University Press.
Oddie, G. (1990) 'Backwards Causation and the Permanence of the Past', *Synthese* **85**, 71–93.
Oderberg, D. S. (1993) *The Metaphysics of Identity Over Time*, New York: St Martin's Press.
Oppy, G. (1995) 'On an Argument about Reference to Future Individuals', *Philosophical Quarterly* **45**, 84–7.
Paul, L. A. (1997) 'Truth Conditions of Tensed Sentence Types', *Synthese* **111**, 53–71.
Peacock, K. A. (1992) 'A New Look at Simultaneity', *Proceedings of the Biennial Meetings of the Philosophy of Science Association* **1**, 542–52.
Percival, P. (1989) 'Indices of Truth and Temporal Propositions', *Philosophical Quarterly* **39**, 190–9.
Perry, J. (1979) 'The Problem of the Essential Indexical', *Noûs* **13**, 3–21.
Plumer, G. (1984) 'Why Time is Extensive', *Mind* **93**, 265–70.
Pollock, J. L. (1982) 'Causes, Conditionals and Times', *Pacific Philosophical Quarterly* **63**, 275–88.
Price, H. (1984) 'The Philosophy and Physics of Affecting the Past', *Synthese* **61**, 299–324.
(1996) *Time's Arrow and Archimedes' Point*, Oxford: Oxford University Press.
Priest, G. (1992) 'On Time', *Philosophica* **50**, 9–18.
Prior, A. N. (1959) 'Thank Goodness That's Over', *Philosophy* **34**, 12–17.
Putnam, H. (1975) 'The Meaning of "Meaning"', *Mind, Language and Reality: Philosophical Papers Volume 2*, Cambridge: Cambridge University Press, 215–71.
Ray, C. (1991) *Time, Space and Philosophy*, London: Routledge.
Redhead, M. (1987) *Incompleteness, Nonlocality and Realism*, Oxford: Clarendon Press.
Reichenbach, H. (1928) *The Philosophy of Space and Time*, English transl., (1958), New York: Dover.
(1956) *The Direction of Time*, Berkeley: University of California Press.
Robb, A. A. (1914) *A Theory of Time and Space*, Cambridge: Cambridge University Press.
Salmon, W. C. (1975) *Space, Time and Motion*, Encino, Calif.: Dickenson.
Sanford, D. H. (1984) 'The Direction of Causation and the Direction of Time', *Midwest Studies in Philosophy* **9**, 53–76.
Saunders, S. (1996) 'Time, Quantum Mechanics and Tense', *Synthese* **107**, 19–53.
Savitt, S. F. (1990) 'Epistemological Time Asymmetry', *Proceedings of the Biennial Meetings of the Philosophy of Science Association*, 317–24.
(1995) ed., *Time's Arrows Today: Recent Physical and Philosophical Work on the Direction of Time*, Cambridge: Cambridge University Press.
(1996) 'The Direction of Time', *British Journal for the Philosophy of Science* **47**, 347–70.

Schlesinger, G. N. (1980) *Aspects of Time*, Indianapolis: Hackett.
(1982) 'How Time Flies', *Mind* **91**, 501–23.
(1991) '"E Pur Si Muove"', *Philosophical Quarterly* **41**, 427–41.
(1993) 'A Short Defence of Transience', *Philosophical Quarterly* **43**, 359–61.

Schuster, M. M. (1986) 'Is the Flow of Time Subjective?', *Review of Metaphysics* **39**, 695–714.

Seddon, K. (1987) *Time: a Philosophical Treatment*, London: Croom Helm.

Shanks, N. (1993) 'Time and the Propensity Interpretation of Probability', *Journal for General Philosophy of Science* **24**, 293–302.

Shorter, J. M. (1984) 'The Reality of Time', *Philosophia: Philosophical Quarterly of Israel* **14**, 321–40.

Sklar, L. (1985) *Philosophy and Spacetime Physics*, Berkeley: University of California Press.

Skyrms, B. (1980) *Causal Necessity*, New Haven: Yale University Press.

Smith, J. W. (1984) 'Towards Putting Real Tense Back Into the World: A Reply to D. H. Mellor's Reconstruction of the McTaggart Argument', *Kinesis* **14**, 3–12.
(1985) 'Time Travel and Backward Causation', *Cogito* **3**, 57–67.

Smith, J. W. (1990) 'Time, Change and Contradiction', *Australasian Journal of Philosophy* **68**, 178–88.

Smith, N. J. J. (1997) 'Bananas Enough for Time Travel?', *British Journal for the Philosophy of Science* **48**, 363–89.

Smith, Q. (1987a) 'Problems with the New Tenseless Theory of Time', *Philosophical Studies* **52**, 371–92.
(1987b) 'Sentences about Time', *Philosophical Quarterly* **37**, 37–53.
(1988) 'The Phenomenology of A-Time', *Dialogos* **23**, 143–53.
(1993a) *Language and Time*, Oxford: Oxford University Press.
(1993b) 'Personal Identity and Time', *Philosophia: Philosophical Quarterly of Israel* **22**, 155–67.

Smith, Q. and Oaklander, L. N. (1995) *Time, Change and Freedom: An Introduction to Metaphysics*, London: Routledge.

Sober, E. (1991) 'Temporally Asymmetric Inference in a Markov Process', *Philosophy of Science* **58**, 398–410.

Spellman, L. (1982) 'Causing Yesterday's Effects', *Canadian Journal of Philosophy* **12**, 145–61.

Sprigge, T. L. S. (1992) 'The Unreality of Time', *Proceedings of the Aristotelian Society* **92**, 1–19.

Stein, H. (1991) 'On Relativity Theory and Openness of the Future', *Philosophy of Science* **58**, 147–67.

Stern, C. D. (1993) 'The Temporal Priority of Causes: Full Explanation or Full Circle?', *Analysis* **53**, 147–54.

Strawson, P. F. (1959) *Individuals: an Essay in Descriptive Metaphysics*, London: Methuen.

Sturgeon, S. (1985) 'A Look at Fatalism', *Auslegung* **11**, 505–13.

Suppes, P. (1988) 'Probabilistic Causality in Space and Time', *Causation, Chance and Credence*, ed. B. Skyrms and W. L. Harper, Dordrecht: Kluwer, 135–51.

Swinburne, R. (1981) *Space and Time*, 2nd edn, London: Macmillan.
(1983) ed., *Space, Time and Causality*, Dordrecht: Reidel.
(1990) 'Tensed Facts', *American Philosophical Quarterly* **27**, 117–30.

Teichmann, R. (1991) 'Future Individuals', *Philosophical Quarterly* **41**, 194–211.

Teichmann, R. (1995) 'Clocks and the Passage of Time', *Monist* **78**, 189–206.

Teller, P. (1991) 'Substance, Relations and Arguments about the Nature of Spacetime', *Philosophical Review* **100**, 363–97.

Thomson, J. J. (1983) 'Parthood and Identity across Time', *Journal of Philosophy* **80**, 201–19.

Tooley, M. (1997) *Time, Tense, and Causation*, Oxford: Clarendon Press.

van Fraassen, B. C. (1985) *An Introduction to the Philosophy of Time and Space*, New York: Columbia University Press.

van Inwagen, P., ed. (1980) *Time and Cause*, Dordrecht: Reidel.

Vihvelin, K. (1996) 'What Time Travellers Cannot Do', *Philosophical Studies* **81**, 315–30.

Weir, S. (1988) 'Closed Time and Causal Loops: a Defence against Mellor', *Analysis* **48**, 203–9.

Westphal, J. and Levenson, C., eds (1993) *Time*, Indianapolis: Hackett.

White, M. J. (1984) 'The Necessity of the Past and Modal-Tense Logic Incompleteness', *Notre Dame Journal of Formal Logic* **25**, 59–71.

Whyte, J. T. (1990) 'Success Semantics', *Analysis* **50**, 149–57.

Wiggins, D. (1980) *Sameness and Substance*, Oxford: Blackwell.

Williams, C. (1992) 'The Phenomenology of B-Time', *Southern Journal of Philosophy* **30**, 123–37.

(1996) 'The Metaphysics of A- and B-Time', *Philosophical Quarterly* **46**, 371–81.

Yourgrau, P. (1986) 'On Time and Actuality; the Dilemma of the Privileged Position', *British Journal For the Philosophy Of Science* **37**, 405–17.

Zeilicovici, D. (1989) 'Temporal Becoming Minus the Moving-Now', *Noûs* **23**, 505–24.

Index

Printed in the United States
68046LVS00001B/47

9 780415 097819